Seeds in the Wind:

from Petit Valley to Staten Island

To my dear Sis
Betty
On your Birthday
You are special
Your name mentioned
Twice in this
Book.
Great Reading

A native of Petit Valley, Trinidad and Tobago, Sue-Ann C. Commissiong is a graduate of the City University of New York. She attended both the College of Staten Island and Hunter College earning a Bachelor's of her own design in a) Creative Writing For and About Women and b) The Anthropology of Race, Politics and Gender. In January 2007, Sue-Ann earned an Individualised Master's in Creative Writing and Post-Colonial Literature at Goddard College, Vermont.

Sue-Ann won the Sylvia Faulkner award at Hunter College for her manuscript *Seeds in the Wind: from Petit Valley to Staten Island.* Academically, and as a writer, Sue-Ann will document her work to impart knowledge she has gained through her life experiences. She would like to travel extensively, using opportunities in this field for gaining more insight and understanding of the world, but moreover, deeper appreciation and respect for the sacredness of all life. She has studied at the University of Hilo, Hawaii, and also the University of Shanghai, China. Sue-Ann has received Honorable mention from Writer's Digest; she has been published by Iliad Press, The National Library of Poetry, Serpentine, Ages & Stages, and The Caribbean Newspaper.

In her spare time, Sue-Ann studies Yoga, Spiritual dances, Samba and Capoeira (Brazilian Martial Arts). She also enjoys outdoor activities such as jogging, spending time with friends, and loves reading and writing poetry. Sue-Ann believes "Everyday becomes more sacred when we move in time with our own special natures, striving for self-improvement and learning from our mistakes."

Seeds in the Wind:
from Petit Valley to Staten Island

Sue-Ann C Commissiong

Seeds in the Wind:
from Petit Valley to Staten Island

Olympia Publishers

www.olympiapublishers.com

OLYMPIA PAPERBACK EDITION

A CIP catalogue record for this title is
available from the British Library.

ISBN: 978-1-84897-017-5

Olympia Publishers is part of Ashwell Publishing Ltd.

First Published in 2010

**Olympia Publishers
60 Cannon Street
London
EC4N 6NP**

Printed in Great Britain

For my grandmother, Jestina, and her seven children
My aunts Angela and Rose,
For my uncles Daniel, Kurnel, Lincoln and Michael,
For my mother, Debbie
And
For Alvin

Acknowledgements

Thanks to my fourth standard teacher, Roslyn Salandy (St. Rose), Petit Valley Girls' Roman Catholic School, Trinidad and Tobago. For my Caribbean heritage and learning throughout my life, I am thankful. To those at Providence Girls' Intermediate and Corpus Christi College, thank you. Sr. Petronilla Joseph, special thanks.

Professor Ed Hack, The College of Staten Island, thanks for your encouragement to "Tell America your story;" my supporting crew at CSI: Fameshia Brown, Tim Gray, Sara Schulman, Gerald Sider, Jim Tolan, Anthony Valerio; special thanks to Alexandra Wagner, Women's Studies department, thanks to all my classmates over 7 years at CSI.

Dr. Nan Bauer-Maglin, Program Director, Susan Fox, Beth Kneller, the CUNY Baccalaureate Program and Thomas Smith thanks for generous support in making my dreams of earning a college degree come true.

Linda Goodman, Paul Grossman, Linta Varghese of Hunter College, thanks for nurturing my efforts in writing, poetry and creative expressions. Special mention to the Women's Studies Department of Hunter College, thanks.

To my family at Goddard College, my initial meeting with Program Director (IMA) Margo Mc Leod, how our early conversations moved me forward, and the silence thereafter leading me to positive action: Tomas Kalmar, Lise Weil, my friend, and also my final advisor Caryn Mirriam-Goldberg thanks for your patience, persistence and insistence in raising me notches upward. To Jim Sparrell and Katherine Towler, thank you. The original Goddard goddesses: Cyndi, Krystina, Hillary, Trish, and Patricia. And to goddesses everywhere, my woman kin: thank you. Larry and Sean thank you.

Special thanks to supporting friends: Pelma Archer, Mary-Ann Carello, Novia Clark, Gail and Neil Dunn, Mary-Ann Espinoza, Betty Franco, John Gillette, Diana Harper, Aliya Hallim, Michelle Hill, Felicia Hutchinson, Ann-Marie Matthews, Yvonne Mendez, Patricia Moonilal, Claudine M. Narine, Patricia Phillip, Alea K. Privatt, Mike Ritchie, Aysha Romney, Lauren Rosales, Lenore Waithe, Leon Wiggan, Trevor Whittingham thanks for listening, understanding, and for believing in my dream.

To my friend of friends: Arden D. Wattley, thank you.

To my American writers and friends: Ted Conover, Edward Beck, Elizabeth Nunez, Natalie Goldberg, Porter Shreve, Anita Shreve, Sandra Cisceneros, and many writing friends I've met across the USA; Dereck Walcott thanks.

To my spiritual leaders and teachers: Omi Cascadu Escayg, Sister Mohini & family of the Brahama Kumari, New York, Mestre Jao Grande, School of Capoeira Angola de Brazil, New York, and also Sylvanna Marquez, my dance and yoga teacher.

Thanks to all my friends and colleagues at the Consulate General for the Republic of Trinidad and Tobago, New York, particularly the Immigration Section. My writing could not be possible without sharing the day-to-day experiences over twenty years.

Anthony thanks for the person you are. To Miguel, my one and only child, thank you for your unending trust in my work; it's been an incredible journey watching you grow and mature.

To the special seeds who passed before me: Lisa Marie Singh, Dexter Anthony Pillai, Brindsley Peters, Alvin Kurbanali, Baba, Rosalia Gocking, Terrance Greaves, Precilla Ali (Tanty Popo), June Bhujhawan (Tanty June), my father, Michael Mohammed and others.

To my family and story characters, special thanks, and while things may have changed from then until now, my stories will always remain; I will not forget how richly you have blessed me.

Most of all, special thanks to my editor, Ms. Gina Bartlett, Sarah Roberts, Esther Harris, Cover designers, Vinh Tran, and all those at Olympia who have supported and brought this work to fruition. I am thankful for our meeting. I look forward to new conversations and writing witty stories.

To all those I have omitted, heart felt thanks and blessings.

Ashe. Om Shanti. Peace. Love.

CONTENTS

There are two ways of spreading light:

to be the candle

or

the mirror that reflects it.

Edith Wharton

Introduction

The island of Tobago

A small island off the north coast of Trinidad, the island of Tobago was the place where you retreated when you needed a rest from the hurried life in Trinidad. Trinidad was fast paced, things were always happening, some party, wedding, or hang out. While life in Tobago was definitely of a slower pace, food was more expensive and there was inadequate island activity. But once you visited you were assured of a refreshing holiday since its main attractions are blue seas, breathtaking views, and good Caribbean local dishes: curried crab with dumplings. Many families visited during school vacations; lovers ventured for weekend escapades. Luckily for us, our mother and stepfather settled on the small island after returning from St. Thomas. At the time you could travel to Tobago either via boat or airplane. *The Panorama* took approximately six hours; the ride over the bocas against high waves was horrendous – narrow corridors littered with sleepy-eyed sea sick passengers puking on the floor beside them. The airplane took about thirty minutes; it was a rough ride. But weighing the two, many opted for thirty minutes of air turbulence as opposed to six hours of discomfort and seasickness.

In the early days my brother, sister and I toured Tobago just like tourists; my stepfather, Alvin, took us to paid beaches, the famous tomb at Plymouth with the unsolved mystery of a woman who lived having been married with children without knowing; tours of the Forts, where battles for ownership were fought by the French, Dutch, and Spanish, and also visits across the countryside towards Charlotteville. The bird sanctuary was a natural habitat for birds; not surprisingly, its property was owned and upkeep paid for by rich foreigners. Among some of the birds that can be immediately spotted are the Cocrico, Tobago's national bird. Together with the Scarlet Ibis the two can be found on the country's Coat of Arms. The Cocrico can be likened to the turkey because of its long skinny legs, and the raucous sound it makes. My favourite birds are the Blue-crowned Motmots. These statesmen-like birds with blue, red and green feathers and a brilliant turquoise and black crown are a sight to behold; Blue-gray Tangers, Copper-rumped Hummingbirds, White-tipped doves, and if you're lucky you occasionally glimpse a White Hawk.

You can see all you need to see of Tobago in one day, that's how small the island is. The population is only a couple hundred thousand, much less than one million, not even half of one million. Most people in Tobago are farmers; they own and plant the land. On Saturdays natives of Tobago bring their produce to the market. They sell fresh pumpkin, *ochroes*, dasheen bush, avocados, chives and more. Ground provisions such as eddoes, sweet potatoes, yams, and cassava are available. Fresh eggs, chickens and meat can be bought; *Mauby* bark, sticks of cinnamon and many familiar spices are also available. The market is an interesting place to visit. You can have good conversations, learn about local medicine and politics, or you can be easily robbed. Market vendors are smooth, they'll lure you with something like "Darling, only $5 a pound, just for you," when the price should really be $2.50 and having not lived there, you would never know. Cunning vendors usually overcharge foreigners or strange looking Trinidadians. I suppose in some ways island people still believe they need to take something back from the "white person" having already lost much of what they owned under their colonial rule.

Today Tobago is not the same place it was when I was growing up. Some of the same people whose ancestors fought for the island hundreds of years ago like the Dutch, French and Spanish, and then conceded to the British, (1889) some of their descendants have over the last twenty years invested in prime property. Mesmerised by the lure of foreign currency, local Tobagonians including the government have sold much of their property and land. As a result, foreign investors have sealed off property from locals. Beach areas, which were once considered everyone's, are now fenced in. Several beachfront properties are now privately owned. Sometimes you cannot even enjoy a long leisurely walk along the beach as when you once felt this was your Tobago. Many foreigners, mostly from Germany, Switzerland, England, and only a few Americans live permanently on the island and own homes. But some visit during the winter months, retreating until spring.

Therefore during September through March of every year Tobago becomes a hot spot for tourism and entertainment. The island buzzes with activity. Especially since this period begins the Carnival pre-season, many mas bands have fête launches, all day beach fiestas, such as wet T-shirt and competitions for steel band and calypso music; luring tourists into a frenzy of partying, drinking and island fun. Some people visit Tobago just for this purpose. If you are not a partying kind of person and want to enjoy a different side of Tobago, you might consider visiting during Easter vacation or May just before summer vacation. You can enjoy less crowded trips to the waterfalls, nature walks and also participate in Harvest day. On harvest day you will be invited into homes to feast locally grown produce and take home fresh fruit and produce.

There are today still some Trinidadians who have never visited Tobago. I don't know why or what about their circumstance that made them not want to see a part of their own country, now only fifteen minutes by air, and three hours by fast boats called *The*

Lynx and *The Spirit of T and T*. It's not the same for Tobagonians because many of them have no choice but to travel to Trinidad on a monthly basis to buy dry goods, see a movie, and take care of personal business. There was once a single movie theatre in Tobago. It became dilapidated and rodent infested. It was eventually shut down because natives took the opportunity to smoke illegal substances, and on occasion were even caught inside the theater mixing private and public business. As it is its own place, Tobago has over many years been neglected by government; one example is the inadequate public transportation system in place. Only recently Tobago received a new fleet of buses which had been promised over many years. There have been many political fights over the years for Tobago to be self governed, but the separation by water from Trinidad made it near impossible not to rely on Trinidad.

In the capital city of Scarborough there is now a newly built wharf with the capacity to accommodate huge ships. The construction of the wharf was long awaited, and it seems millions were well spent. There is also a lovely view from the harbour area looking out to sea; the entire space gives the impression of a street fair as small concrete kiosks make it possible for vendors to congregate and sell local arts and crafts, trinkets and homemade sweets. Thanks to private investors from Trinidad a brand new movie theatre, Movie Towne was built not even one year ago. It is only a few minute's drive from Scarborough.

Tobagonians are country folks; they live incredibly simple lives, take care of their families and attend church service on Sundays. Today, while much has changed in Tobago's physical landscape and means of living, much has also remained the same. The lure of a fun loving filled vacation surrounding tranquil azul waters still entice many. The promise that Tobago can evolve into one of the Caribbean's premiere tourist destinations might still be in the making.

Chapter 1

Debbie

I never resented my mother for leaving my sister Susan, brother Ricardo and me. My parents married in 1960. In the three years following their union, they had three children, my brother being second and me the last. Any brief recollection of early childhood including father, mother, children and happy home was when we first lived in a small modest house that stood at the top of a steep hill, next door to the Clarke's house on Church Street, Petit Valley. Mr. Clarke was a taxi driver. His wife Ms. Sylvia and my mother became friends, talking out many hours of the day. They were a family with four children Bernadine, Kathleen, Martin, and Pascall who befriended us. While sparsely decorated, our home was furnished with one Morris rocker, love seat, single chair, lace curtains, small dining area and one bedroom. I remember jumping from chair to chair with my siblings, when someone fell over the round wooden table and broke my mother's vase. As we scampered out of living room, and hid ourselves, an angry voice declared: "Wait until your father gets home!"

Petit Valley Girls' Catholic School was the first school my sister Susan and I attended. It was conveniently located minutes away downhill, opposite Miss Cinder's parlour, next to St. Anthony's Roman Catholic Church on Morne Coco Road, with Petit Valley Boys' Catholic just a few yards away on the opposite side of our school. Miss Alexander, a short stubby woman with large round glasses, was our first introduction to learning. Vaguely I recall the early days at school, crossing streets with tiny hands holding on to other tiny hands in a long line, singing "Old Mac Donald had a farm..." But, I could easily picture small brick houses, and the concrete standpipe more than half way down Church Street, the same standpipe under which we bathed, splashed, and giggled, filling mouths with water, then sputtering over each other under a changing sky. When the Valley's evening sun disappeared into varying hues of tangerine sheets covering Morne Coco Road, we made several trips to the standpipe carrying plastic buckets of water. I watched as older siblings carried the load, trying to balance filled buckets on soft skulls, while at the same time joking around with the Clarke children. Whenever rain poured, we were happily drenched, looking up to heaven with wide-open mouths, and loosely hanging tongues.

Our family life at Church Street was short-lived as my mother left not long afterwards. We did not grow up together. I heard people say my mother had deserted my sister, brother and me, wandered off from her husband with another man, settled on an island, and hadn't looked back. The little memory I had of our father living with us was also short-lived. My father worked at the United Grocers in Port-of-Spain, the capital city. But before my mother's leaving, she moved our entire family to my grandmother's home in Crystal Stream, about two miles from Church Street. I must have been about seven.

My father remained with us only temporarily in Crystal Stream. My grandmother Tina, a widow with seven children including my mother, raised me. Growing up at my grandmother's, I sometimes overheard many distasteful things about my mother. Behind closed doors, in hushed voices adults discussed in more detail events of her leaving her husband and children. Whether these were true rumours or not, I never heard her respond. I didn't care about what I heard, could not. She was my mother and I loved her. There still remained a blur in my mind for a couple of years when I heard nothing from my mother, and little mention of her name at home – adults sworn to their own silences, children learning early how dangerous it could be to venture into "big people's" talk. In 1970, when I was almost eight years old, I wrote to my mother my first letter:

10th October, 1970

Crystal Stream

Petit Valley

Dear Mummy,

I hope you are well. Mummy I am now in Standard 3A. I am trying to keep up with my work as you told me in the letter. I am going to make my first Communion on 1st November, 1970. How are things in Tobago? When are you coming? I want you to bring me a doll and a tea set, also a pair of earrings, please.

Bye, Bye for now. God Bless You.

Your loving daughter,

Sue-Ann

My mother, Debbie Evangeline, stands at five feet nine inches, with hazel eyes and short cut light brown hair. Her sapodilla skin complements a slender body and she smiles easily. Growing up in Trinidad, and eventually when she contacted us, I wrote many letters to her asking when she would return. She didn't address that question. Over the years, I related day-to-day events sending her riddles, prayers and jokes, and told her how much I missed her. Often, I asked her to send me money to purchase school supplies, clothing, and other necessary things. She always sent the cash.

From the time I was about ten, we started visiting with her after learning she had settled in Tobago. These trips were scheduled around school vacations: Easter, summer and long holiday weekends. My mother bought the ticket. My grandmother's niece, Aunt Janet took us to Tobago; we drove for one hour from Petit Valley passing Beetham Highway that smelt of burning garbage, speeding past Kirpalanis' Roundabout, St Augustine, then turning right at Piarco towards the airport. My Aunt Janet was the best lady driver I had ever seen, crawling on Wrightson Road, alongside large overloaded trucks, taking over lanes of traffic on the outside lane, gazing through rear view mirrors, telling off crazy drivers. She was careful and, at the same time, fearless. It was something to look forward to – packing, driving in her scarlet Datsun – watching her foot move, dangle, moving from gas pedal to brake to brake and gas again. But it was especially exciting pulling off the highway to buy local snacks like curried mango, red plums, and doubles, or if my mother needed, fresh vegetables. I remember seeing tiny scantily dressed East Indian children aged about seven to twelve years old with sorry faces, dodging traffic, weaving bony bodies between vehicles trying to sell drivers bundles of *bodi*, chive, bottles of homemade pepper sauce, and plastic bags of *ochroes*. We could see their families in the distance sheltering from too much heat under galvanised makeshift stalls, safeguarding homemade goods and produce. Seeing these things, I often wondered, ...*I thought my family and I were the poorest of poor.*

In the early 70s, Tobago was about thirty minutes by air. The *Arawak* was small, cramped, and got its name "shake and bake" as in "shake and bake a chicken" because that's exactly the kind of ride we got. Thirty-five minutes later, we embarked with dinner mint in hand, which lovely looking local airhostesses distributed. A few years later under national airline BWIA, replaced older airplanes with high-powered jets making the trip in 12-15 minutes. These new aircrafts were named after Hasley Crawford, Trinidad's first gold medallist at the 1976 Olympics; he won the hundred metre dash. Another jet, the *Buccoo Reef*, was named after the majestic coral reef situated in Buccoo, Tobago, a small fishing village. There was yet another jet named after *Janelle Penny Commissiong*, Trinidad & Tobago's 1977 representative at Miss Universe, who grabbed the crown. I remember seeing her gorgeous face flash across the TV screen with a hibiscus flower stuck behind her ear, and a dimpled smile. My sister and I were certain she'd steal the crown. Her face simply lit up like a 100-watt bulb, I thought, *Wow, what a beautiful woman*! When she returned home to Trinidad and Tobago as Miss Universe 1977, and later set up a boutique on upper Frederick Street, I begged my high school friends to stop by.

Her boutique "Janelle's" was located in the capital city of Port-of-Spain, just past the Royal Jail, a few yards away from St. Mary's Boys' College. It was on our way home – those afternoons when noisy teenage girls walked in groups, unbraided their hair, put on lip gloss, met with other high school girls, followed boys to the taxi stand at Independence Square where we congregated, and often slurped milk shakes from Dairy Queen at street corners. Before getting downtown, whenever we got to the famous dress shop, after walking from Belmont Circular Road, half way across Queen Park Savannah, down Frederick Street, we just stood outside, hiding ourselves from the window view between dressed up mannequins, peering, winking at her, smiling, and me showing signs of deep admiration. Standing there, I often compared Miss Universe 1977 with my mother. Janelle was physically and beautifully elegant and intelligent. Winning the crown, she'd travelled the world, met famous people, and was revered by many. My mother was smart, but was still confined as a woman in many respects – still trying to find her way in the world. Outside the shop, we watched Janelle's assistant shooing us off, sending angry looks our way, gesturing us to keep walking.

During weekend visits or longer trips to Tobago in August, my mother and I talked away days, with her evading queries about her returning home. I imagined my mother was particularly skilled in the art of talk by the way she cunningly deflected conversations about she and my father. Still, I did not understand. We spent some Sundays lying half naked on sandy Black Rock beach, so named because of the black sand, soaking up blazing sun, and jade saltwater, listening to the ocean, roaring waves and laughter from a distance. I liked Black Rock because it was simply beach and sand without man-made additions. Jogging the entire length two or three times, gave me power, control – just me – wind, sand, sea and God watching over me. It was at Black Rock that gigantic female leatherback turtles swam lengths from deep ocean, risking their lives as in earlier years poachers often lurked nearby waiting for them to crawl up on to the beach, raping them of their exotic shells, and slaughtering them. Whenever turtles were not caught, they lay eggs, carefully concealing them with sand, before again heading out to sea. I marveled at such magnificence whenever we got glimpses, but was equally saddened every time we stumbled upon black crows nipping away at bloody turtle remains.

Gradually, conversations between my mother and me deepened. I was honest about everything. We lived apart, so I had nothing to hide from her. We talked about boyfriends, parties, youthful temptations and indulgences, freely sharing stories. She knew me and understood that like her, I wanted to taste life. I shared with her that the first party I attended, was my friend Shelly Welsh's 16th birthday, held at their home in Pearl Goodman Avenue. I was 14. I confided that the rust cotton blend maxi dress Aunt Angela made for me fitted perfectly – it fell upon skinny shoulders emphasising developing breasts, wire waist, long black hair falling past my back, stray strands over chest. When Shelly's brother Vaughn asked me to dance, it was my very first slow dance to Marvin Gaye's "Let's Get It On". I told her how I felt like Jell-O mixed with condensed milk in his arms, and also liked the way his hands gripped my curves, that when he moved his hands up and down my spine, I was in a crazy panic for the rest of the afternoon. I shared with her that when we played kiss catch later at the party,

I let him catch me just for the kiss. I shared with her that I was in love with Vaughn Welsh after discovering we shared the same birthday, December 24. I believed we were made for each other. Vaughn and I flirted with each other. I saw him every time I went over to Shelly's place, and then on our walks home from church. But not long afterward, Shelly and her family moved away from our neighborhood. So Vaughn and I grew apart. Seeing less of Vaughn Welsh, my mother gone, and my father living with another woman, I realised love was always changing.

My mother and I spent our time together wisely talking, cleaning or cooking. My mother taught me how to prepare local dishes, make fruit cake, and offered tips about household chores. I usually sat on the kitchen counter with a pen and notebook in hand, jotting down homemade recipes as she dictated from memory, while preparing specialty dishes. My mother seldom used measurements, averaging ingredients, trusting instincts to process, making perfect hops bread, coconut bakes, and pies, anything she wanted. I noted some favourite phrases her mother had repeated to her, witty sayings like, "You can bring a horse to water, but you cannot make him drink it". My mother's advice to me was simple, "Darling do your best, leave the rest". While some lines evoked laughter, she quickly pointed out the double meaning. Sitting closely, I received instructions about looking after my grandmother, helping out at home, and stern warnings about not being rude. My mother constantly reminded me of the hot pepper mouth I owned, cautioning that my words stung, and I should be careful. She also lectured me about maintaining sound moral values emphasising simplicity, and, as far as I could see, she tried to live a life that matched her words. That was good enough for me.

Whenever school grades dropped, my mother encouraged me to try harder and not give in. She told me that it was only when one delved past her limit, that one would realise how much more potential there was inside, waiting for discovery. She was there for many school functions and graduations. She stood proudly beside me both in success as well as in disappointment.

II

During my teenage years, my mother and I became closer through our letter writing. I remember when my first love tragically passed away in a tractor accident, on the north coast hill of our island. I was devastated. He was just eighteen. I felt my world and everything surrounding it had exploded before my eyes, that there was no hope. The agony of this pain could neither be effaced nor eased. I pondered: *Why was life so unfair? Where was God? How could I ever love again?* My mother travelled from Tobago to be with me. I could not have known then, but it was her strength upon which I relied. She came to me and wiped away pouring tears. She stood beside me among bereaved family and friends on that sad December morning, the day of my love's funeral, and held my hand. It was she who first told me that "...time was a healer..." and "...All things pass..." She was there when I most needed her; it was all that mattered. She gave me new courage to endure life and accept its challenges. Through the experience of death, I took her hand in mine; we became friends.

I never knew when my mother was ill or whether she was broke; I didn't know whether her bills were paid or if she was just having a bad day. I don't remember her being upset or angry with me for any length of time. She never told me those things, but I often saw pain in her eyes. I saw that she was working extremely hard day after day, that from a distance she was doing her best to take care of her three children. My mother was once a pupil teacher in Trinidad. She later became a store clerk, working for a large chain store, Kirpalani's Group. When she moved to Tobago with my stepfather, she worked for the same store. It was the largest department store on the island. No doubt, most people shopped there; everyone knew my mother. She bought us nice clothing. Especially for me, she purchased gorgeous lingerie, cotton sundresses, Easter and Christmas outfits, fancy socks and school necessities. My sister, inclined to being Tomboyish, got jeans and tees, and was equally pleased. It was through my mother's actions that I started to understand and accept her love. I could not separate myself from her without her knowing. She always had encouraging words to say, and reminded me that God was in charge of our lives, and only He knew best.

My respect and admiration for my mother continued to grow. Though we lived separately, she dreamt my dreams along with me, constantly assuring me that whatever my goals and aspirations for the future, I could achieve them, little by little, and that the sky was my only limit. She was not afraid to let me know that there were sacrifices involved, mistakes to be made and, of course, lessons to be learned. Born on April Fools Day, I saw that my mother was no fool. She let me go my own way, be my own person. She let me live.

III

Over the years, I started to put pieces of our lives together. I learned that my mother had been through some very hard times. When she and my stepfather left home (he also left his wife and family behind) they travelled to St. Thomas where they stayed for a while – I suppose to quiet things down because angry spouses would have been searching for them. About one year later they returned and discreetly settled on the island of Tobago. The only person who knew about my mother's whereabouts was my Uncle Daniel, her brother whom my mother always trusted. In Tobago my mother and stepfather both had to start life over from scratch, find new jobs, a place to live and worry about how their children were growing up.

Not long after settling in Tobago, my mother made contact with us and soon we were able to visit with her. She and my stepfather rented a house with three women, Molly, Zalina and Annlyn; they all had separate rooms, and were decent people. The area in which they lived was called Pomp Mill. Their boyfriends visited often and whenever we all met, we were one happy extended family, mostly sharing beach outings, cooking and our lives. Always searching for cheaper rents, they moved from Pomp Mill to Whim, and later when the three women each married their boyfriends and moved on with their own lives, my mother and stepfather moved to Fort Street. Everyone remained the best of friends. It was later in my mother's and stepfather's lives that they purchased a home in Buccoo, a small fishing village near Mount Irvine Golf Course, west Tobago.

Eventually the two settled down; my stepfather sold insurance to make a living. At Kirpalanis, most Tobagonians knew my mother and many loved her; they often described her as the tall, fair skinned woman with green eyes. I remember my mother relating an incident that happened on the job, where she was sitting on a high chair while the Manager, her boss, sat on a lower chair. My mother told me how irate he became the moment he discovered he had to look up at her, the employee. She told me he felt insulted looking up to her. In the same breath, she warned me about boss and employee relationships, telling me to always be careful, give them their respect and make them feel important. While I told her it was a two way street, and bosses ought to respect their employees, I realised she was passing on to me her life's lessons.

My mother seldom spoke a word about my father. By the time I was a young woman, I heard that my father had beaten her, and she had fled from him. As harsh as truth ever is, she unwillingly confirmed this several years later. In 1985, my stepfather, Alvin, took my mother to Europe, where at Gretna Green, Scotland, acting spontaneously, they had a "shot gun wedding". The day was

June 16th; the couple lived together for seventeen years. It was my mother who proposed, since she had often in the past declined my stepfather's offer. What made my mother take my stepfather's hand that day I cannot exactly say, except I knew the two were inseparable. The marriage was legalised; I was glad they married; they deserved each other in all the ways that count as love.

Only one year later, just before my own marriage, my stepfather had been admitted to hospital for minor surgery (gall stones). We were assured the surgery was a success. But what baffled us, was that every time we visited my stepfather in the hospital, his condition seemed to be worsening. Yet, nurses said he would soon be discharged. This never happened. I visited with my stepfather to tell him I finally passed my driver's test, after failing the first time because I didn't make the three point turn. I was so excited to tell him *I got it this time.* Lying there, his faint smile troubled me immensely. My stepfather passed away on the hospital bed on July 6, 1986. Moments before, he had requested what would be his last wish, "One Red Solo, and a chicken roti, please." He had held my mother's hand tightly, I suppose intuitively understanding, he would never walk out of the hospital with her.

In late September of the same year, almost three months after my stepfather's death, at twenty-four, I married a wonderful young man as had been planned. I wore my mother's precious diamond necklace and earrings that her love, my stepfather had given her. My mother assumed a familiar trance-like state at our wedding, the same state she had sustained when my stepfather died months before. She was present in body for support, but she could not be expected to be over his death. Pictures prove this fact. Her eyes were lifeless and empty. She had lost her soul-mate. My stepfather was simple, deep and wise. I missed our together times. He was the first to tell me years before, if I documented our family's history it would make the best seller's list! Still, my mother reminded me "...that good things happen when we are fully engaged with life..." She celebrated with me.

IV

In 1987, while I gave birth to a healthy baby boy, one of the most wonderful events in my life, my mother stood at my side holding my hand repeating, "Breathe, breathe, you'll be OK..." During intense pains, labour and excitement of the moment I had screamed at her, "Breathe, breathe..." She forgave my frantic outbursts. *Could I possibly ask more of a friend?* When my son was only about six months old, my mother whispered to me. She advised if I wanted more children I should consider it then and not delay the process, since my husband and I were young and fit. Only years later would I come to recognise her truth.

Debbie has become a significant part of my life; I don't have to pretend when I'm around her, she knows me. We've cried many times together, been angry or just kept silences; it is wonderful to share this kind of intimacy with her. It is good to have a friend, but when that friend turns out to be my mother, it's an even greater adventure and blessing. My mother has taken time to love me. She has moulded and shaped me. She has taught me. Whenever I think of her, the words written by John Addington Symonds come to mind, "...In a land of sand and ruin and gold, There shone one woman, and none but she..." These words remind me of a woman, Debbie Evangeline, my mother, the best teacher I've come to know.

Chapter 2

Tina

Tina is her name, short for Jestina. And when it was called she answered at once. "Yes, Daniel," walking over to the table where her eldest child was having his meal.

"What is this?" he sternly asked, slightly raising his bald head, and pointing a finger to something on his plate.

"Well, I tried to make you something different, you're always complaining about eating the same food on the same day of every week," my grandmother stammered.

This exchange continued like a recurring decimal, on and on, before my grandmother, frustrated, hurried off to the bedroom. "Now I have to get ready for mass." She emerged in less than ten minutes, dressed in a cotton knee length dress, sandals, and a dab of red lipstick, clutching a lace veil, Bible, rosary, purse, and making sure she had change for collection. She went to church sometimes, twice a day, at 6am, and 6pm, three or four times a week, and also on Sundays. Some evenings we went together. Our parish priest, Father Cyril ward, was Irish, friendly and concerned about his parishioners. Years later, the Church of Nativity was built only a five minute walk from our home, just after crossing Crystal Stream Bridge. Crystal Stream Bridge had its own folklore associations, stories of *Soucouyant* and *La Diablesse*, lovely ladies of the night who lure men and you never hear from them again or they become crazy. They were said to be dead people luring you into their world. These stories made us afraid of venturing out alone at nights without being escorted.

My grandmother whom we seldom called Ma, Granny or Grandma was perfect. We liked the name Tina. She was small and fine boned with strong, over-worked hands. They were, I learnt over time, an extraordinary gift. Her face was small, narrow, her eyes big and dark, inside deep sockets. She had wide hips. But I especially loved taking care of her hands. I clipped her fingernails, and then applied Jergens Hand Lotion. I massaged each finger, pulling them up to my face, guiding them gently up and down my cheeks. On some Saturday afternoons, when the sun towered, my grandmother took a long, cold shower. Afterward, she put on a nice flowered cotton dress, applied some face powder, and only a smudge of red lipstick, the same lipstick she always used. Then we both sat in the gallery to soak up some sun and soothing breezes. Clipping her nails, I glanced up as humming birds danced towards small coconut trees, later settling over bunches of ripe bananas, darting in and out neighbouring yards. In March, just before the April rains came, full blossoms of yellow *poui* trees sprinkled green hills.

While her feet were still damp, I looked forward to cleaning and clipping my grandmother's long hard toenails. Kneeling at her feet, towel-drying, playing around, wanting to polish her toenails in nice colors, but she never let me. If she shampooed her hair, I waited for it to dry, straight and shiny in the sun. Afterwards I brushed it, tweezed out some gray hair, checked for lice, and then combed it into a small neat roll, which I pinned up in the middle of her head, French style. We slept in the same bed so closely, you couldn't tell there were two people. Often when she questioned, "What are you going to do when I'm gone?" Nestling under her arm, my head upon her bosom.

"You are not going anywhere, and besides, I will go down in

the hole with you!"

I was born in the sixties in the Caribbean islands of Trinidad and Tobago. Separate islands, but one country. The lovely islands lay seven miles from the South American mainland at the mouth of the Orinoco River, off the northeast coast of Venezuela. As far as history goes, it has been recorded that the name Trinidad comes from "La Trinity," meaning the three. When Christopher Columbus spotted the breathtaking mountains, he thought of the Father, Son and Holy Ghost, and praying to the three he named the island.

Most Indian families in Trinidad grew up in the countryside, Central, and South Trinidad. They were surrounded by lush vegetation, seasonal flowering trees, rivers, and other families who planted and tended the land, raised pigs, cows, goats, and chickens. We lived about half an hour from Port-of-Spain, in the suburbs of Petit Valley, not far from the enlivening waters of Blue Basin Waterfall, Macqueripe and Carenage, the last two being part of the Caribbean sea. Even though I couldn't swim for many years, I loved the ocean. The water, I felt, was too deep for my understanding. I thought it overpowering, it could take me somewhere far, never to be found.

Our minds were as simple as the clear water. Our thinking was as free as everything that grew green and wild, unlike most Indian families, whose children were confined inside the boundaries of tradition, religion and culture. In Hindu families, husbands were chosen, and bargains made for a daughter's hand in marriage. In Muslim tradition, and according to the laws in Trinidad, a man chose one wife, but it was understood within such communities he could have several. Our family, on the other hand, always had choices and chances. We learnt Catholic things, went to Catholic schools, and understood once we were young women, we had to marry, have children, could not divorce – that once we lived within those boundaries, happiness followed. So we picked our own husbands, just as we went from garden to garden handpicking green pigeon peas that were plentiful and ready. So from quite young, whenever I had to, I learnt how to make my own decisions based on what I knew, and I grew to rely mostly on the voices I heard inside of me.

Though my grandmother practiced Catholicism, I knew she had not been born Catholic, but was baptised in the Catholic Church. She said her prayers in a tiny sealed off area in the kitchen, where she often lit candles and put lovely fresh red, pink and white roses from her flower garden into a cup of water. My family was Hindu and Muslim; my mother's side was Hindu, and my father's, Muslim. My ancestors came from Northern India to work as indentured labourers in the sugarcane fields, in the old colonial days, when our islands passed through many foreign hands of ownership: French, Spanish, Dutch and British. Around 1801, after war between Spain and Britain, Trinidad became a British colony and remained under colonial rule until August 31, 1962, when it became an independent nation, under the scholarly rule of the Prime Minister, Dr. Eric Eustace Williams.

At first, my family had a glimpse into Hindu ways, performing *pujas* in our backyard, then attending *Hosay* celebrations in praise of the gods. I remember standing in the kitchen beside my grandmother, holding on to her dress, my right thumb securely tucked inside mouth, watching her. I would repeatedly mumble her prayer words which she recited in Hindi. As our lives became more entwined in the Catholic Church, a natural consequence of colonialism, and when friends visited our home regularly, the home-made shrine was removed.

My Aunt Angela's husband, Gunness Singh, built a new altar inside my grandmother's bedroom just above our bed. It was adorned with white lace, statues of the Virgin Mary, St. Anthony, and St. Martin. A crucifix with Jesus lying dead stood mounted on the wall near a photograph of Pope John Paul II. These images made a great impression on my childhood as my grandmother and I recited the rosary, repeated psalms, read Holy Scriptures, learning through prayer and worship, to trust God and his angels in everything. I knew that if I lost or misplaced something that I could pray to St. Anthony. Still, I would stand at the space in the kitchen wanting my grandmother to take my hand, begging her to invoke her dead family. Instead she warned me, "Little girl, what are you looking for? There is nothing there anymore!"

My grandfather was tragically killed – knocked off his bicycle by a truck. The accident occurred on the Western Main Road in St. James, the closest town from where we lived. He cycled there each day to do his trade; he was a goldsmith. From their union, my grandmother had seven children, three girls including my mother and four boys. Just before my grandfather's death, their eldest son, my Uncle Daniel was taken out of school when he was exactly 14 years and 11 months old. He got a job at the United Grocers, a large supermarket in Port-of-Spain, because my family was just that poor. When my grandfather died, the responsibility of taking care of his mother, five siblings, and later, two nieces, and one nephew fell squarely on my uncle's shoulders. A collection of exactly $26 was taken up at work to help my Uncle Daniel and his family cope with the loss of the head of their household.

Tina had been unlucky to lose a handsome husband. To make a living, my grandmother sold snowballs made from shaved ice, and made market errands for a number of people. Growing up in that household, watching my grandmother work hard, and later observing her four sons leave the house from about 6am each morning, not returning until sunset, I quickly realised that a man brought income into the home – the woman was expected to take care of everything else. Even then I saw the equation was unbalanced, because my grandmother was not only responsible for putting food on the table each day, but also for ensuring that every dollar she received was used wisely. This was not easy! No one ever taught my grandmother how to budget or manage a household. She occasionally muttered, "Only those inside the kitchen will feel the heat." Indeed, the heavy responsibility of taking care of seven children demanded much; over time, it overwhelmed my widowed grandmother. What was even more startling for me was she almost never complained. Seeing all the things my grandmother did, and endured, I was certain of one thing: it was <u>only</u> from God that she got her strength.

I tried to help my grandmother with household chores, but could not keep up with her. By 7am, before we could afford a washing machine, every garment was hand-washed and hung out to dry in the early morning's sun, which she believed was best. Around eleven, she had returned from the market with fresh fish, fruit and vegetables. Another uncle, Michael, picked up our dry goods at Eversley's that averaged $56 weekly. This is exactly how I wrote the list:

10 lbs. Rice

5 lbs. Flour

5 lbs. Sugar

3 lbs. Potatoes

½ lb. New Zealand Cheddar

¼ lb. Baking powder

¼ lb. Curry

½ lb. Salt meat

½ lb. Salt

1 lb. Red beans

1 lb. Lentils

1 lb. Split peas

½ lb. Black eye peas

1 bt. Oil

1 tin Carnation milk

1 tin Condensed milk

1 tin Peas & Carrots

1 Box Matches

1 Box Mosquito Destroyer

Our kitchen was small, cozy, welcoming in an L-shape. There were as many cupboards as pots and pans. Above the kitchen, I stuck a sign "Tina's Kitchen." There was a large white top and bottom refrigerator, and a big square sink. The concrete floor was painted red, which we, bent on hands and knees, hand-polished every Saturday afternoon, and then used an Electrolux floor polisher to buff. The walls were brilliant gold with white fancy blocks. A rectangular table covered in colored vinyl, which we changed for festive occasions, had four cushioned chairs.

In my grandmother's house, we ate good home-cooked food. Our kitchen smelt of freshly minced seasonings or orange-peel tea. My grandmother assured us "If we had nothing else, we should always have a plate of food to offer someone." By noon, whenever I greeted her, and checked the kitchen for my breakfast, there might be a huge iron pot of ox-tail soup cooking with black-eye peas, dumplings, pumpkin, *ochroes*, sweet potatoes, yams, and dasheen. There might also be another pot on the back burner. After I lifted its hot handle, dropped it quickly as the steam flared into my face and the hot cover scorched my fingers. The sharp smell of curry filled the kitchen. While pointing a scrawny finger to some spot on the counter, my grandmother gave me a stern look, "Miss, look at your breakfast, over there!"

"Thank you Tina," I'd tease, wrapping my hands around her

shapely waist. While I sat at the table, or sometimes closer to her, on top the white, tiled kitchen counter savouring hops bread dripping with homemade guava jam, licking my wrist as jam trickled down my hand, she continued her cooking, singing "How Great Thou Art" Her voice was mellow, the lyrics, broken, and because she didn't breathe deeply enough to hang on to higher notes, she often skipped into loud hums, peering at me from the corners of her eyes.

Tina had a male companion who visited her sometimes on weekends. Darren was a short, Madras looking man, with deep-set, black eyes, and a frightening stare. But he was soft spoken, and had a good smile. On these visits, he usually brought her a bag. From it she removed fresh tomatoes, or *melongene* (eggplant), ripe plantains, assorted pieces of candy that I longed for, and always something special for her hidden deep inside another small canvas bag. She loved *tolum* (candy made with molasses), and coconut turnover. After munching on some treats, she and Darren sat closely in our living room on an old Morris chair hugging, laughing, and chatting. Whenever Darren spoke in whispers, my grandmother's giggles sounded like playing puppies. I was sure she would marry him, even though they never went into the bedroom together.

Unexpectedly, Darren died of natural causes. My grandmother took it hard. I watched as her glint of happiness faded because once again fate had betrayed her. She didn't sing for a long time, and she didn't talk much. Day after day, she quietly went about her usual business around the house. Whenever I looked into her dark eyes, they seemed dull – empty. I knew she missed him; she didn't have to say it. Many times I caught her unaware, staring into nothing over the kitchen sink, occasionally wiping away tears she carefully tried to conceal from everyone. After Darren's death, my grandmother never entertained another male friend in our home.

My grandmother loved to share. Whenever the only Julie mango tree in our yard bore fruit, we picked dozens of the green mangoes. Under the tree, she made separate piles, counted at least four to a heap and declared, "These are for Tanty Popo... (my grandmother's second sister)... "These are for Yvonne..."(my grandmother's niece); "These are for Tanty June..."(her youngest sister); "These are for Uncle Harry..." (her brother); "These are for..." She called each of our neighbors, friends and family by name, and made a pile for each. I had the job of going from house to house to deliver mangoes. Everyone knew that when kept in a brown paper bag, or wrapped in newspapers, the mangoes ripened sweetly.

Many days, I sat outside on a big rock shading from blistering sun under our guava tree searching for – admiring my grandmother, watching her busy in the kitchen, imagining her strong working hands. She would often look out at me through the louvres, slightly tiptoeing, yelling, "You think I'm not seeing you, you little miss!" She was always keeping a keen eye on me.

Chapter 3

My Aunt Rose, Otis Redding and Bob Marley

From afar, voices echoed… heavy galloping like racehorses… I wasn't sure – coming from the yard, up the front steps towards our house.

"Leave me alone! I'm going!"

I immediately recognised Rose's voice.

"Leave me! Leave me please, Daniel!"

This time, her voice was broken, teary, full of painful emotion. Then, "You are not going no f… place!" was the harsh response, a man's voice.

I remember when my grandmother Tina's youngest daughter, Aunt Rose left home. She was about seventeen. She had carefully planned the day. It happened one bright, sunny Saturday morning when Tina went to market. Everything seemed as expected, except – what was about to unfold.

I quickly ran from the kitchen, through the living room, just in time to see my Uncle Daniel with fiery eyes, and his three brothers in some kind of confrontation. I couldn't tell what was happening. They were all standing before the long glass door that separated the living room from the gallery. I noticed Rose's friend, Gaston pulling her away from family. At the same time, Daniel stood in the middle like a serious roadblock. My head was spinning. Everything was happening too fast. While I had been standing in the living room and watching the rectangular wall clock tick, to me, time was stuck.

Daniel had his hand in a big fist. Another cousin scampered in to help. Together with his three younger brothers, they tried to restrain Daniel from losing his wit. I hardly watched the commotion, covering watery eyes with both hands, peeping only when I dared. For some reason, Rose wanted to leave with Gaston, and Daniel was trying to protect his little sister. Still, I could not understand why. *Why this fighting? Where was Rose going? Why did she want to leave?* A series of whys flooded my mind. Pieces of a gigantic puzzle flew about, questions without answers moved quickly inside my head, swirling around my mind.

I walked towards my family. Motionless, I stood in a corner near the bannister. I saw it all, heard the ugly words. It was the first time I had ever heard Daniel curse. He mentioned the word *chop*, which I had always associated with wood. It was also the only time I had seen Daniel pick up the cutlass, the same one he'd used so many times around the house to cut grass and overgrown hedges with, in a violent mood. Its blade was long and shiny with smooth edges. The word *afraid* could not explain what I felt. While no one was badly hurt, just some bruises and swollen knuckles that fight created a deep, uncured wound in my family's history. Without listening to any of her brothers' protests, Rose left home with Gaston.

Rose was a beautiful young woman; about five feet, had black hair that flowed past broad shoulders and reached just under her buttocks. She wore it in one long plait neatly coiled behind her head, secured in place with bobby pins. She had big bright, light green eyes, wore glasses and had smooth, tanned, thick legs that emphasised a full figure. She always had a serious expression, tried to be tough, and to me, after she left her family behind, lived through the events of her life as if she was paying for some crime she believed she'd committed.

The name Rose was no longer common around our home. If spoken at all, it was usually in whispers, especially in Daniel's presence. She visited her mother, and other siblings during the day when Daniel was at work. Though I would see her, I couldn't speak with her for long, since she herself must have felt cut off from the family. She didn't say much to me either, and usually walked around with her head lowered.

Time passed. Around the neighbourhood, gossip spread. It was rumoured that Rose, a nice Indian girl from a good Indian family, spoilt her life – ran off with a worthless black man. *What kind of future would she have with someone who was unemployed? Where would they live?* These were only a few silent echoes heard everywhere. Once you belonged to our family, you heard it.

About eighteen months later, Rose tried to conceal the fact she was carrying Gaston's child inside her slightly swollen belly, which no one had yet noticed. As news of her pregnancy became more obvious, she endured looks of contempt, and tried to mask the shame by pretending her life was great. She hardly complained to anyone, and lived a secretive life.

I wasn't surprised when she named her first-born son Otis, after one of her favourite singers, Otis Redding. It was at her home that I heard "Sitting on the Dock of the Bay". The infant was the colour of a half ripe cherry with light green eyes, tiny nose and mouth, and short stubby toes. About two years later her second son, Donavon was born. It was also at her home that I first heard Percy Sledge sing, "When a man loves a woman" and Bob Marley's "Who the cap fit". While cleaning, she danced around their small wooden shack, and when my sister and I visited with her, we followed her around using a mop stick as our microphone, chanting after her, giggling silly. She played those songs over and over from vinyl records on an old-fashioned stereo set. But Rose dared not share a dark secret with us. At least, not yet.

One holiday, the day after Christmas, my sister and I visited Rose. We found her bruised and broken; a gash to her forehead sent blood rushing down the corners of beautiful eyes, down swollen red and blue cheeks. Her eyes turned different colors, hair out of place, clothes torn. She trembled with pain and fear. Her boys, Otis and Donavon were in the bedroom crying, the older comforting the younger.

We went with her to the West End Police Station on the Diego Martin Main Road, not far from where they lived. The station was a huge, unpainted concrete building, a scary site. When we walked inside, I shivered, and grabbed for my sister's hands. There were long empty corridors, which did nothing to erase my fear. Some people passed us, seemingly busy with their own problems. Three policemen ran ahead of us, and then we saw one large, wooden desk. Together, we approached. My sister and aunt quickened their pace; I stumbled behind, fear numbing each step. Reaching the desk I overheard, "Miss, we can't do a thing to help your aunt, domestic problems must remain at home! Go home! Take your aunt home!"

That was what the uniformed man sitting at the desk had said. His voice was harsh, and cold just like the building. A group of policemen hanging close by quickly dismissed us, using their hands to wave us off. As we turned our backs, I recalled how some of the policemen talked and laughed as we passed, murmuring that this was not their business, saying that they were certain "this woman look for the blows." The experience made me feel like nobody. Later we took her, with the help of a friend, to the Port-of-Spain General Hospital, where she had more than ten stitches. That night, our Aunt Rose made my sister and me promise not to tell anyone. It was a hard promise to keep, the burden of which gnawed at my conscience.

I always believed there was something in the lyrics that my Aunt Rose repeated as her mantra; it took years to figure out. In the secrecy of her life, her children's father beat her. "Just a push here and there, nothing to talk about," she had once admitted when my sister questioned. "Don't tell anyone," she begged. Maybe she felt this was her problem, since she was the one who'd left home; she accepted that she had to live with the choice of her youth. This was the grave secret she hid from everyone in her family, except those like my sister and me, who, on occasion, stayed at her home, and got a real glimpse into her life.

Months after the incident, with fresh images still floating around my mind, I might have just turned eleven; I began putting more pieces of Rose's life together. I realised suffering the way she did, listening to music was perhaps the one thing that gave her some hold on hope. She also had a fine sense of humour, another one of the many faces she comfortably wore. I remember her telling her boys in frustration, "If I only had more sense. I would have planted two Julie mango trees instead." Puzzled, I asked, "What do you mean, Rose?" Jokingly, she replied, "Because all now I would have been sucking sweet ripe mangoes instead of having these worries!"

We burst into contagious laughter. But when it trailed off, and we were left separated by the intensity of our silences, I knew that Rose had done her best to raise her two sons, and that she cared for them more than her life.

My Aunt Rose and I did not become very close. Time did not permit it. In her eyes I was just a child – *what could I have possibly understood*? In my mind, she was my aunt, and I loved her, but what could I say to her seeing all that she'd suffered through? She was good to me because it was her familial duty; my mother being her big sister, family looked out for each other. Over the years she attended the PTA on my behalf, signed report cards, and took me to school bazaars. Rose taught me many girl things. When she believed I was old enough, she lectured about condom use, then later showed me without any hint of embarrassment when I menstruated, how to insert a tampon. As years passed, and I matured, I understood more. I realised that Rose resented herself for having left home so early. But more deeply, in some way, she became uncomfortable with the fact I had developed a strong and loving relationship with her mother. I was the one who lived with her mother, and four brothers.

Still, Rose got me my first real job in the same company in which she worked. She was a jewellery-maker, a craft inherited from her father, and she worked in a jewellery factory. The owners had seven retail stores located in malls across the country. Rose told her boss she had a really smart niece who needed a job, "She's not at all like me," she admitted to Mr. Rawle Jeffrey, one of the three owners of Colibri Jewelers Company. What my Aunt Rose meant was I studied books, not boys, I was the young one in the family who went about life as if I had a goal. She meant I wasn't like she – who had defied her family, left home unmarried, ran off with a man who was a car mechanic and who abused her, then later became pregnant. What Rose didn't know about me was that I always thought she had guts. I never told her given the chance, I would probably have done the same thing she had done, had I believed I was in love, and had found the man of my dreams, I believed she was much too hard on herself.

What I learnt about my Aunt Rose and our relationship was the fact that no matter what happened, and while understanding usually takes a lifetime, people do what they have to in order to survive. Sometimes, we do it unconsciously, doubting, but still hoping things will work out. It would be years later in the 1980s with Gloria Gaynor's hit, "I will Survive", making waves when my Aunt Rose mustered enough courage to change her circumstances, face the consequences, and try to build a new life for herself and her children. She blasted the song from her car, at home, wherever she was *liming* all the while strengthening herself for the road ahead. Marley's classic, "Three Little Birds", also lifted her heavy spirit when we heard her singing. In her we saw new strength. My Aunt Rose and I may not have been best of friends; still, I was lucky because we had developed a mutual respect for, and a tolerable understanding of, each other's ways.

Chapter 4

Angela

After a couple of years, my grandmother's fourth, Aunt Angela, married, and left home in Petit Valley to start a life with her new husband. The year was 1969. We had the wedding at home. My grandmother, our family and friends cooked the food. We had *roti*, chicken, goat meat, mango, *channa* (chick peas) and potatoes, all of it curried. The wedding was small. Angela made me the most beautiful little dress I'd ever worn. It was lime green with long, puffy see-through sleeves, fitted at the waist with a short flared skirt, exposing skinny legs.

My Aunt Angela was a soft-spoken adolescent who attended Corpus Christi Girl's Convent, and did all the things a pretty little girl was expected to do. When she graduated from Corpus Christi's Convent, my aunt started working as a secretary in the same school she attended. In her long, flowing white wedding gown, Aunt Angela looked like the angel she's always been. Just over five feet, she had long slender legs; she was light-skinned with sea green eyes that changed shades. Her make-up was strong, eyes lined with black kohl. For most of her wedding day, and from behind curtains I stared at my lovely aunt as she walked around smiling, talking to guests, thanking them for attending her wedding. She seemed perfect, and in that instant my Aunt Angela became my heroine; I wanted a life fashioned like hers, marrying a decent man, having a good job, and gaining the chance to live life on her own terms in hope of starting her own family.

The man my aunt married, Gunness Singh, was an extremely talented man. He built houses; he was also a plumber, cleared overfilled sewers, and dug new ones; his job was important, and he was contracted for more than one year at a time. He wasn't boastful, but his voice projected a strong demeanour. It was the way he explained himself about building and repairing things that let people understand he knew what he was talking about. He talked about money, making more money, and having enough to support his wife and family; he wasn't overly ambitious. It was the early 1970s, and money flowed just like oil in Trinidad. Jobs were not hard to obtain, families were building larger houses, buying expensive cars, indulging in extravagances such as taking vacations to exquisite places, and people were making a good living. My aunt's husband was no exception, and for a number of years he provided for his family. On occasion my aunt also had excess income to treat us to a shopping trip, or a church bazaar.

In the early days of their marriage, my Aunt Angela took us to the movies. She usually rounded up some of the kids in the area, and made it an outing. At the box office she got the tickets, popcorn and Coke, and led the noisy, anxious, under twelve group inside the theatre. I remember some of those events such as the time we went to see *The Flying Nun* starring Sally Field, *The Sound of Music* with Julie Andrews, and Aunt Angela was also the one who took us to see our first Indian movie, *Mother India*. After that movie at the Astor Cinema, I realised how deep Indian history and culture delved, how families prearranged their daughter's wedding, how difficult this choice often became for both parties, how true love was tested, perfect love near impossible to find, and always loss, family feuds including some tragedy of death. I felt glad we didn't live inside those boundaries, but still emerged from the movie theatre with puffy swollen eyes, everyone laughing calling me "Cry baby."

In their union my aunt and uncle had a first born son they named Anthony Reginald, but then their second child, a daughter, Lisa died of jaundice when only a few weeks old. When they brought her home from the hospital, she was dressed in a delicate white flowing dress lying still inside a small wooden rectangle box. It was the first time I'd had seen a baby lying helpless inside a box. Her eyes were not tightly shut, but softly. She was angelic. My aunt took the loss of her first baby girl hard, but at the same time her strength as a woman started to emerge. We only imagined the extent of her pain having carried the baby full term, feeling movement inside her belly, knowing an infant was growing, witnessing the birth of a daughter, holding and feeding the precious infant in her arms, only to lose her quickly. She quietly mourned, cried and moved on. Not more than one year later, she gave birth to her third child, another baby girl, Stacey-Ann Tessa Marie. But I grew up never forgetting the delicate baby girl lying still inside the box. I remembered when we laid her more than six feet inside the earth, covered by loose dirt and darkness. I learnt early life, was something we could not take for granted; it was a gift given by something greater than any of us, and those of us who got to live beyond our first few months, had the chance to give it our best shot by choosing to live a good life.

The couple eventually had six children. With each pregnancy my aunt worked harder, and it seemed nine months took much more from her physically than she had bargained for. But she didn't believe in using contraception; she believed each conception was a miracle. In many ways I came to see she was right. Around her fourth pregnancy, my aunt worried doctors; they warned Aunt Angela about considering contraception after pregnancy, but she wouldn't listen. She was cautioned about not being able to carry another full term pregnancy even though her health was at severe risk. It could be a choice of her life or that of her newborn's life. But my aunt put her trust in God, and stood strong behind her convictions. As she grew thinner, family members spoke with her, tried to convince her to listen to her doctor, but she wouldn't change her beliefs. She quietly took on her circumstances, and didn't complain.

When she became physically strained, and financially burdened raising her children, coping with another pregnancy, her job, a husband who over the years became irresponsible, and her family, I don't remember hearing her complain. Often whenever we visited her late at night, she would be washing, hanging loads of clothes, cutting up chicken preparing for the next day's meal or ironing bundles of clothes; she was always on the move. *Hail Mary full of grace, the Lord is with thee, blessed are Art Thou among women and Blessed is the fruit of Thy Womb Jesus...* was the first prayer I linked to my aunt whenever I reflected on her ways as a mother, Catholic woman, secretary, and my loving aunt.

After graduating from high school, and attending Corpus Christi College, I got a close up glimpse of my Aunt Angela's world at work. It was her first and only job. She was the school's secretary, friend, and confidant. Students rushed to visit with her, explaining their problems; teachers were drawn to her gentle spirit and calm approach to things. The school Principal, Sr. Petronilla Joseph, and my aunt had been best friends since they attended the same school together. Sr. Petronilla left Trinidad to study abroad and join the order of Carmelite sisters, only years later to return, and find my aunt still working at the convent that later turned into a college. They continued working together over many more years, and their friendship also grew deeper. My Aunt Angela remained loyal to duty, and a faithful friend. Today she remains a treasure, living life with us the best way she knows. She is a good mother, and wife; those who know her are lucky to be in her company.

I spent weekends visiting with her, and the children. With the first three, Anthony, Stacey-Ann, and Stephan, her hands were filled. There was always much housework, cleaning, cooking, taking care of the children, going to church, and spending time with her family. If we didn't visit on the weekend she dropped by on Sundays at my grandmother's. We loved the children; and they quickly became spoilt. I enjoyed getting them dressed up, taking them to mass on Sunday morning, playing games with them, going for ice cream later in the day, and being sad whenever later in the evening we had to take them home to their mother. My relationship with my aunt was always changing for the better. Once, when I was babysitting Stacey-Ann, she accidentally rolled off the bed and hit her head, hard. My Aunt Angela was mad; I saw fire steadily rising in her eyes, but I also saw that she understood something more – that I, too, was a child.

By the time my Aunt Angela had her other three children, Andre, Kerry-Ann and Michael we celebrated three more cousins, and finally no more babies for Aunt Angela. My Uncle Kurnel and his wife Ann-Marie had five of their own, my Aunt Rose two, and Uncle Lincoln had one; we had fourteen first cousins in all. Together with my mother's first three, my grandmother had seventeen grandchildren. Since we were the eldest of all our cousins by about ten years, we were called upon to take care of them. It was always a good experience because we got to watch T.V. for long periods, have snacks that were not usually allowed, and in the absence of adults played wild games.

My Aunt Angela is left handed; people say left handed people are artistically inclined. My aunt's gift is sewing, cutting pieces of cloth free handedly, and creating articles of clothing. I often brought her fabric, requesting her to stitch up an outfit. I brought the fabric, thread, zipper and matching buttons early Saturday afternoon, needing it for about nine that night. I might help with house chores or babysitting, while she busied herself on the table. Explaining what I wanted to wear was not difficult, some mini skirt with matching strap top; my aunt sketched what she believed I wanted. Then she cut the fabric without using any form of paper patterns, and sewed together pieces of cloth into a beautifully made garment. While I appreciated my aunt's talents, and turned up at parties in a one of a kind outfit, my friends marvelled at her abilities. My aunt made me my communion dress, confirmation dress, and whenever we attended weddings; she made us dresses. I imagined she and I made a good twosome designer team; we could become rich if I managed her business, and designed outfits; she'd cut and sew. We'd create an original boutique of handmade clothing, and invite friends and family to buy pieces of clothing. But standing in her way was always the issue of time.

Aunt Angela's abilities were put to the test when she was requested to design and create my wedding dress. At first she didn't know whether she could handle the task. After mulling it over for a few weeks, and when I mentioned to her I wouldn't ask anyone else, she consented and immediately started to draw her own gowns. Her eyes lit up, and she did a kind of jig she always did whenever she was happy. I assured her she could do it. After searching various bridal magazines, taking a sleeve from one dress, neckline from another, skirt from another and so on, my aunt and I pieced together a full wedding dress. She had a good idea of what she was going to make, including a fully beaded skull cap attached to a long flowing white veil that fitted in the centre of my head.

Before getting married and for more than six months, I had the opportunity of watching my Aunt Angela work from the designing stage, to the final creation of my wedding dress. There were long nights, lots of coffee, and hand sewing. We had good talks about what to expect in a marriage, in between fittings and laughs. She was my perfect role model. I didn't have to look to Hollywood. As far as I was concerned, my Aunt Angela was a genius. She also loved to sew. In between her making my wedding dress, she was interrupted time and time again to sew garments for people such as; nuns' articles of clothing, working suits, and school uniforms. My aunt moved steadily from task to task, never once mentioning how tired she was or even if she was fed up with all our requests and demands. My wedding dress was perfect. On my wedding day, my Aunt Angela only had to make a few minor tucks around the waist and chest area because I had lost a bit of weight with all the running around involved in preparing for a wedding. She had already anticipated this, and had in her possession needle, thread, buttons, and beads handy. Aunt Angela proved just how a specially gifted person she was with an incredible heart.

My Aunt Angela's relationship with her siblings was also a special thing to observe from the distance. She had two sisters, my mother her older sister, and their younger sister, Aunt Rose. My aunt was good at putting things together, and keeping relationships from falling apart. I noticed the deeper she got in to her faith, the more she had to offer as a sister. She could be trusted. If my mother told her something in confidence it would stay there; she didn't have to tell anyone what she knew for the sake of being the news carrier in the family. My mother turned to her time after time for advice whenever she had to make a decision, or if she just needed to talk. In fact my Aunt Angela was the most discreet. She forgave my mother for leaving her family behind years ago, and did whatever she could to take care of her two nieces, and one nephew. For this we, my sister, brother and I, can never thank our Aunt Angela enough. Her relationship with her four brothers was also special in the way she related with each one. She had the most respect for her older brother, my Uncle Daniel, who had taken care of the family since he was eleven. She developed close contact with my uncles, Kurnel and Lincoln, and in particular with their youngest sibling, my Uncle Michael.

The characteristics I describe about my Aunt Angela were the parts of her that stood out before me while growing up in her care and company. These were parts she couldn't tell stood out before me – that became etched in my memory – that during lonely periods of my life whenever I closed my eyes, I had good dreams, each day became more bearable, making me want to grow up, have plans for my life, and dream bigger dreams. My Aunt Angela was a wonderful source of inspiration in my life; without knowing how she helped me survive. She walked through my life giving me courage and faith, moving me beyond what I had dreamed possible. Her quiet demeanour has been my hope, my comfort in times when I didn't think any of it made sense. Thinking about her journey, her experiences, and her joyful acceptance of her circumstances, filled me with pride for having known her, having loved her, having her be my aunt.

I hope this writing gives justice to the person my Aunt Angela is; I know everyone in our family will agree. She has been a pillar of goodness, hope and wisdom for those who come before her. Her sincere understanding of life, and being nonjudgmental strengthens me, helping me create my own sense of wisdom. Because she tries to live what she has become, and this has most to do with her faith and trust in God, today she radiates this inner self. In my own spiritual quest for truth and understanding, and the path I have chosen, Aunt Angela has not judged me. One year she shared with my mother a dream she had had about me. She said in the dream she saw me walking along a path...alone. It was a long hard path, and it was so difficult, there was no smooth walkway. It was unpaved, stony, and uncertain. There were no streetlights, and no one in sight to help me through. But my aunt related how I kept on going, walking and pushing ahead. From that time I realised my Aunt Angela saw me living in my own sense of truth. I had been travelling the journey alone. Now I knew she was there with me. I believed her prayers and good wishes were always with me and the choices I made.

The first time I returned to my homeland after living in the USA for several years; my Aunt Angela made my homecoming one to remember. She came to my grandmother's place, and made the bed putting on fresh cotton sheets; knowing how much I loved flowers, she put a bouquet of freshly cut flowers including roses and red ginger lilies on the table with a welcome sign "Welcome home Suey, We love you." Reading the handwritten words, and seeing the vibrant tropical flowers brought tears to already wet eyes. She made sure my granny was looking nice, her hair combed and she was wearing a cotton dress. My mother was also present; she came from Tobago and waited for my homecoming. My Aunt

Angela didn't know it, but it was her effort and love that most affected me. It instantly hit me what being home meant; I felt the weight of living eleven years without the closeness of my family being gently lifted from my shoulders. Aunt Angela went out of her way to make me feel I was home; she helped peel layers of loneliness away. It was her gentleness I remembered long after returning to New York when harsh winter months numbed me.

This was love, pure and simple. It was the simplicity of everyday living we craved for, yet so easily forget. It was what we sometimes spend a lifetime chasing and never find. Each time I travelled to my home country, I was reminded about the life I once lived, and the thing that mattered most, my family. That I survived eleven years living in America, without having the chance to revisit home was amazing. That together with my family I lived in a foreign country bringing my values and culture, giving the best of what I had to offer, learning what I had to, assimilating into the norm of life here was also amazing. That returning home to Trinidad, while my family still could not, was torture. But we coped, and just like my Aunt Angela taught me, we learnt courage, and lived in hope.

My Aunt Angela visited with us here in the USA about three times over seventeen years. She grew to appreciate the sacrifices we made for a different life. We openly spoke about our plans and circumstances in the USA. She offered advice and encouragement reminding us of the main reason we left Trinidad and came to the USA. It was to build a "better" life for our son, so he could have opportunities for learning we didn't have – so that he could build a future with more options and open himself to fulfilling his deepest ambitions. She assured us of her prayerful wishes for prosperity. I shared with her the fact I didn't want to retire in the USA, that whenever all our resident papers were finalised, I intended to return to my homeland, and continue working as a writer in the community. Most of all, I wanted to return home to be closer to my grandmother. My Aunt understood this sentiment more than most, since she knew how attached I have been to my grandmother, and how difficult it has been for me living without her.

In my forty-fourth year of life on this lovely Planet Earth, I recently shared with my Aunt Angela how much I yearned to return to my homeland. I told her I once believed I could come to America, take what I needed and leave. But it wasn't that simple or easy. There are too many things happening at the same time; things take time. This vast and often lonesome place has become my home away from home; New York City with all its complexities and opposites has grown on me. While we used opportunities that came our way to make a good life, and I am thankful for the people and events that came before us, seventeen years is a long time. Severing ties with the land and people that have nurtured my growth process, and made me into a stronger more unique individual is a tough call.

My Aunt Angela listened to me; she once again assured me of her prayerful wishes for me, and the choices I now face. She understood my internal struggles and told me I will know what I have to do when the time was right. She recognised changes in me and she willingly accepted this as part of who I have become today. Once again she has not judged me; her gentleness has been my constant companion. She nudged me forward in my work and writing. She acknowledged I was once again changing with each new season, and in many ways often without words, she has walked the distance with me. This is the thing that gives me a deeper understanding of who she is as a person – the thing I cannot touch. This is the thing that allows me to see her as she is without her having to answer questions about her life, her favorite colour, place or food. But I once learnt just like millions she loved Elvis Presley, could dance Rock and Roll, and adored Rock Hudson. So I knew from early she had taste for the best.

As her life has taken on new struggles with five grandchildren, my Aunt Angela continues to do what she knows best. Her love, natural instinct and expertise with children, having successfully raised six of her own together with nieces and nephews, remains something to watch in awe. She is present. She still suffers silently, moves around joyfully, and gives much more than she ever receives. She now spends some summer months visiting holy cities and places, being a true disciple of the faith she was raised in. She still prays wholeheartedly, and for such steady faith and conviction, she deserves my deepest respect and admiration.

Chapter 5

Kurnel

My Uncle Kurnel, middle name Clarence, my grandmother's third, was fair-skinned with compelling blue eyes. He was tall and lanky, endowed with a perfectly pointed nose, and short jet-black hair, and always resting neatly on his forehead was a slick, greasy Elvis Presley curl. He was nicknamed "The Dude" mainly because of his manner of dress. I had learned early that my uncle Kurnel was aloof. Distant and quiet. He never joined us for a game of Snakes and Ladders or Monopoly. The only times he allowed me to hug him were on Religious holidays, his birthday in July, and at Christmas.

Kurnel was neither an unfriendly guy nor was he outspoken. He quietly took in life's experiences, and loved sincerely. None of my uncles finished school, let alone had any chance of receiving a college education. Our family's reality was quite simple; we were a poor family, trying to survive. In the time that we lived together, Kurnel had had several jobs, including working at a number of grocery stores, selling insurance, becoming a marketing agent for wholesalers, transporting and promoting new products. His one weakness though was his devotion to the bottle of rum brewed in Trinidad and Tobago later becoming known as "the Spirit of Trinidad and Tobago," which, even as a child I concluded was the main reason for his changing jobs so frequently.

My uncle's first girlfriend was young, lovely, and lively; Molly was tall and slender, with a face the shape of a small football. Sadly, this relationship didn't last too long as she migrated overseas. Although it is said, "Absence makes the heart grow fonder," and even though my uncle loved her, circumstances prevented any permanent union. Afterwards, in June 1975, my uncle married his second girlfriend, a marriage that bore five children, and for me, it meant another set of first cousins to love. Kurnel fell in love after courting his pick for nine years. Her name, Ann-Marie Williams; her body was curvaceous; she wore dresses just above her knees, and had a butt that bent corners long after she'd passed. On weekends, having attended 6pm church service at St. Anthony's, another Catholic church about one and a half miles from where we lived, Ann-Marie and Kurnel came home together, talked and laughed with us. Then she and her love, my uncle, found a cozy corner under dim lights in the gallery to share each other's company. They made the ideal couple. Ann-Marie was lovely and deserving of him, I thought. I admired them; enjoying moments my grandmother asked me to serve them glasses of *Soursop* or *Mauby*, and freshly made bread pudding.

Years before my Uncle Kurnel's marriage, and eventually, when all three of my grandmother's daughters no longer lived at home, my mother being the first to leave, then Rose followed by Angela, I remained in my grandmother's care, a little girl growing up among my grandmother's four sons: my uncles, Daniel, Kurnel, Lincoln and Michael. I was special and spoilt. Everyone knew this. It wasn't surprising when each Sunday morning I anxiously waited for Kurnel to wake up. He didn't have to look very far for me; I followed him from bathroom into the boys' bedroom, and watched as he opened the termite-eaten wooden closet where he reached for hanging pants. From pockets he retrieved and handed me a bunch of dollar notes, then sent me to Don's parlor.

"Little girl, go across the street, and you already know what to get us, right?" his eyebrows wavered.

"Right!" was always my eager response.

The bright red bills in hand excited me. Barefooted, in shorts and T-shirt, with long uncombed hair falling past middle of my back, I raced down concrete steps, uphill towards the front of our home. Hearing kiskadees hum behind me, and along the way, I wiped my fingers against rose petals and leaves wet with dew, gently patting moisture unto my newly pierced ears, loving the tingle cold droplets of water made on sore earlobes. Older aunts told me that night dew was a natural healing element. They were right.

Across the street, there were not many people around, just a few returning home from Sunday morning mass. Early morning sun was still rising in the distance, air moist; my bare skin felt warm under the coolness of Petit Valley's morning breeze. Crossing, I passed Eversley's grocery shop. Miss Lynette and her husband Marion owned it, and had her sister Irma employed there together with one village boy, Dave Singh. What impressed me was that Lynette and Irma could accurately add up a copy book page of numbers in seconds just like a calculator. Sometimes small groups of people on the opposite side of Morne Coco Road were gathered, waiting to buy fresh beef from Mohammed's. He transported meat from the country every Sunday morning. By eleven he was completely sold out and closed.

Walking along the partially quiet Crystal Stream Avenue towards Morne Coco Road, I'd also see some families, Christians just returning from mass. They were dressed in their Sunday best: men in shirt jacks and soft pleated pants; women wearing pastel-coloured dresses that fell below their knees, wide-brimmed hats; girls in brightly coloured outfits, hair braided and tied at ends with polka dot ribbons, with matching socks and shoes. On their way home, they'd also stop at Don's to pick up bread, pastries, candy, cold drinks and cigarettes.

Donald Lutchman was a tall, pleasant, Indian man who was

married to a woman named Lola. They owned the parlor and bar, "Lutchman's" about one hundred yards near the curb where Morne Coco Road cuts Crystal Stream. They were well respected and revered for their mouth-watering curried beef and chicken rotis. They lived next door, had a family of three daughters and four sons with whom we grew up. Over the years our families became closer particularly through death, with Don and his wife first losing one of their daughters, Glenda, to sickness, then Don himself died. Later, one of his handsome sons, Keith, who many girls wanted to marry, died in a car accident. From a young age, I saw that while death took people away, it also joined long lost friends and families.

In Don's, I impatiently waited my turn, rocking my body from one side to the other. There was no line, no attention being paid to who came first, just bunches of people shouting for items like, "One sandwich loaf;" "Two tamarind balls and four pepper plums;" "One pack of Broadway and a box of matches;" and then I'd chime in, "One red Solo, and one tub Cannings ice cream, any flavour except chocolate."

If it were Saturday, I'd hear "One chicken roti with plenty pepper to go..." "Four beef roti, no pepper, hurry up, my wife is waiting... Two beastly cold Carib Lagers." I'd hear similar requests over and over as people came in and out for lunch. I'd also see Don's wife, Miss Lola who usually worked in the kitchen running to and fro managing cooks, wrapping roti, and putting orders together. Again, if it were early Saturday evening, there might also be a certain lady seated on a stool outside Don's, selling the hottest black pudding with hops bread and also plastic cups of souse.

Her main customers were men who frequented Don's Rum shop. There might even be a group of Baptist women called Shouters, depending on whether or not a full moon was expected. First sign of their presence was a loud ringing bell. This ringing bell confused villagers as the only other time we heard a loud bell was either at school or, whenever WASA drove by warning us because of road repairs, the water supply would be turned off. This group of Shouters made quite a disturbing picture to a little girl – with heads tightly wrapped in varying shades of cotton cloth, from greens to reds to whites. If they were assembled near the curb, in front of parked vehicles in Don's parking lot, I made sure to pass behind them, often edging myself into the street. The long white dresses they wore tied at the waist with several pieces of brightly coloured cord worried me. Most of all, their bulging eyes, and serious, penetrating looks on the Shouters' faces made my heart palpitate. Usually, one woman carried a big iron bell, continuously ringing it with such force that I had to cover my ears and bend my head. At the same time, other group members shouted praises, clapped hands, chanted and sang hymns such as, "Lay your burdens down" or "Go tell it on the mountain", swaying their bodies in soulful rhythms. What frightened me most was that I had no idea to *whom* they prayed. No one ever bothered to explain anything to me. *Was it the same God that my family and I prayed to? Was it Jesus Christ, the chosen Jew, who saved the world? Was it Lakshmi, the Hindu goddess of light, beauty, riches and love? Allah? Or were there other gods?* It was rumoured that Baptist people practiced obeah, lit black candles, and performed ceremonies on deserted beaches, across the country, late at night, baptising individuals in cold seawater to welcome them into the group. Passing them, I cautiously proceeded.

But it wasn't Saturday; I didn't have to worry about the Shouters' presence, and Sunday was calmer with Don effortlessly managing the entire parlour operation, standing statesman-like at the cash register, taking in cash, giving out change, raising hands to point out which customers to serve, and giving instructions to his children, who each had different tasks fluttering from customer to customer, learning from experience. From where I was standing, I couldn't help looking into the adjoining Rum shop that was separated only by a counter, wire meshing, and a different entrance towards the other side of the parlor. I got quick glimpses of men who had probably spent most of the night sitting there, drinking themselves into stupidity, men who might have spent the previous night outside closed doors, then returned when the bar reopened the following morning. These were men who were afraid to return home to angry spouses because they had spent most of their weekend earnings on alcohol, gambling, other women, and listening to music. This music matched their sorry lives, and it echoed from an old jukebox. I heard songs such as Bob Marley's "No Woman, No Cry" or the Mighty Sparrow's (Calypso King of the world) "Drunk and disorderly". I didn't dare gaze into their eyes; they were ugly and stale, sleepy-eyed faces too drunk to recognise anything or anyone, much more to care.

Somewhere from behind the buzzing in the parlour, and recognising my voice, one of Don's sons, Brian would come rushing out to my aid. Brian was thin, and had an awkward walk; he wore large glasses, and was nicknamed "Professor." He'd pack the paper bag nicely, wink at me, I'd pay him with a flirtatious smile, wait for my change, then be on my way. When I turned to leave, chiming continued, "Two butter bread please"; "One Nutrament…" In that same spot, and, while making my exit, wives came by to drag husbands home, while other men teased young women calling them names like "sexy thing", or "sweetness", making rude passes at them.

On my way home, I'd be sure to find something I hadn't paid for inside the bag, my favourites being Smarties or Tunnocks Caramel Wafer. It was Brian's way of expressing interest. While traffic was scant, the corner was still dangerous. Once, while returning home running, ice cream in one hand, while with right hand holding change, I tried to prevent flying hair from getting into my eyes. Attempting to dart across the street, I suddenly heard a loud screech of brakes behind me. I didn't bother to look back because the thrill of returning home with ice cream and soda was the only thing on my mind. I didn't yet realise that in an instant, I could have easily been run over.

Life in Trinidad is simple. Trinidadians are a "no problem" kind of people. You don't need an invitation to visit someone's home. Especially on the weekend, you could just walk into a friend's home after church and say, "Well, I was passing through the neighbourhood, and I smelt your pot... What are you cooking today?" You'd then be invited to stay and *lime,* hang out, maybe help out until the meal was ready. After having a full serving of local dishes, "Trini" music, and old talk, visitors will usually be offered some food to take home. At that moment, they'd then exclaim, "Gosh the whole day pass already, I didn't even realise that!" indicating that they had perhaps overstayed their welcome.

Sitting in the gallery, my Uncle Kurnel was always delighted to see me return carrying the brown paper bag, which meant as requested I'd gotten all the items. As I excitedly hurried up the front stairs, grabbing the black iron rail for support, he with outstretched hands stood up, took the bag, and, then when I extended my hand towards him, he'd motion, "Keep the change." Sauntering to the kitchen, my uncle carrying the brown bag, me hopping near his heels, only with feigned gesture of composure, we'd notice my grandmother who would be the approving silent observer. My uncle emptied the already melting tub of ice cream, licking soiled fingers, and poured the bottle of sweet-drink into a big silver bowl. He first blended them with a spoon. Next, with a wooden stick he mixed and mixed the two ingredients into a frothy, effervescent, thick liquid. Licking my lips, and twitching from side to side, I waited. He added a dash of Angostura and vanilla essence then mixed again. Finally, he poured the mixture into two large glasses, one for him, and one for me.

When he headed for the gallery, I skipped behind. Undisturbed, we sat together, he on a single corded chair, facing the lush green mountain of Petit Valley towards Simeon Hill, where the Mighty Sparrow lived, and me, on the wooden floor with my legs spread out long, soaking up his face. We drank without saying a word. Ours was a familiar love built on quiet understanding. I often stared into his warm blue-green eyes, which grew warmer and shone silvery in the wake of sunlight. His face softened just a little during our Sunday shake ritual.

Chapter 6

Lincoln

Love didn't come easy for my Uncle Lincoln. My grandmother's fifth child, he was born on December 21, 1948. Looking more like my grandmother, small framed and handsome, he was just over five feet with deeply set brown eyes, wore size six sneakers and always left a distinct trail of Mennen cologne behind him long after he'd gone. A handsome man, he wore crew necks tucked inside close fitting pants, usually Lee jeans. His coffee skin was smooth, his hands neat. For many reasons I could not have understood, he seemed cautious with life, walked slowly and did things in his own time.

Following closely in the footsteps of his siblings, Lincoln attended Diego Martin Boys' Catholic school, and did not finish school. None of my grandmother's children received college education; our family was simply too poor and concerned with immediate means of survival, fate having dealt an early blow when my grandfather died. Instead, my uncle, like his older brother my uncle Daniel, also had to seek early employment. He worked at Suares, a small supermarket located just minutes away from home, before a fork in the road that separated Petit Valley from Diego Martin. Most days he walked. At the grocery, he learnt to cut slabs of meat to perfection having had only one accident I recalled, when his hand was badly severed, he had to get many stitches, and was forced to stay away from the dangerous meat cutting machine. When I examined the job of meat cutter, I realised how much caution was needed for cutting meat, with both hands confronting a hissing machine equipped with long sharpened jagged blade, while simultaneously separating pieces of sirloin, chunks of beef or lamb shoulders. It required skill that could be learnt, but more importantly, it demanded concentration. My uncle was an excellent meat cutter, perfecting slabs to his liking. During recession years when Suares experienced financial trouble, eventually closing its doors, my uncle got another job at Petit Valley Supermarket on Morne Coco Road. He remained employed there for another couple of years. Somehow my grandmother's children were never unemployed for any length of time, and even though we lived in poverty, there was never any shortage of food.

My uncle Lincoln dated a number of lovely girls, and after his first heartbreak, in March 1970, he quietly married a young woman, Theresa Guppy, whom he could not take his eyes off. She was a tall, dark-skinned, lean woman with thick shoulder length hair, looking like someone with Amazon ancestry. In the beginning, they lived at her parents' home at La Puerta Avenue, not far from where we lived, which made visiting easy. On June 6, 1971, she gave birth to a daughter, Sandra Donna-Marie. Our families gathered for special events over shared meals. By the late '70s, when I suppose things were becoming too complicated at his in-laws' place, my uncle made another change. When he started a new job at a ceramic and tile factory, my Uncle Lincoln built an apartment, plastering walls, laying down tiles and painting, himself. The apartment was situated downstairs in my grandmother's house in Crystal Stream. He was content when it was completed and his wife and daughter could move in with him.

Socially, my uncle often played cricket on weekends or joined others to play all-fours (cards). If I were tagging along, I'd sit on the icebox, mix drinks or run after loose flannel balls out on the field. My Uncle Lincoln brought home our first puppy and named him "Blondie;" he was white with some brown spots. When Blondie died, Lincoln dug a hole in the backyard near banana and peas trees, buried him, said his silent goodbyes over the grave, and soon afterwards brought home another puppy called "Patches", as in the song "Patches" by Clarence Cater. He fed, walked and loved Patches. Life for my uncle's family seemed normal, and by the time Sandra started kindergarten at Mucurapo Girls' in St. James, I had many babysitting hours whenever Lincoln and Theresa went to the movies, or spent nights out with friends. Sandra was like a cute baby toy to me. I loved bathing, dressing, and combing her spaghetti-like hair. Then I took her for afternoon walks, picking roses from hedges. Sometimes, when my own wickedness set in, I pinched her chubby face and arms making her look like an over ripe pommerac, watching her cry herself silly to sleep.

Theresa prepared delicious meals and cleaned the house, but she never pretended to be the staying kind of wife. She appeared unsettled and openly expressed this to many in our family. There was a noticeable restlessness in her eyes that I recognised as some kind of longing for anything other than what she currently had. It wasn't that my uncle was cruel and didn't take care of his family; it wasn't even that she didn't love him; it was simply that restless longing taking control of a woman's soul. Alone, she often sat on the back steps staring into space. Whenever someone questioned, she didn't make up stories, but instead casually mentioned she wasn't there to stay.

I wasn't surprised when one rainy morning, Theresa, who was always her own person, declared that she was going to America to join her family, who had migrated there sometime in the late '60s and '70s. It was the same time when it seemed to me that everyone or someone in everyone's family was leaving for America, England or Canada. Back then I told myself I could *never* leave my home to settle in a foreign land; more so, I would never leave my grandmother. Everyone was shocked, could not believe how Theresa came to be leaving or the reason why she was leaving. The most obvious explanation people rumoured was because of some man. Theresa drank her black coffee on the back steps, playing loudly the Commodores hit song "Easy." I remembered her chiming in loudly to the lyrics. When I heard her chanting the same words every Sunday morning over a period of time, I realised she was serious about leaving. She and I were born only one day apart from each other, December babies; she was December 23, and I was December 24. My uncle's wife left with their only child in May 1978. I think that in the pain of his wife's leaving and taking their only child, my Uncle Lincoln grew, in some ways, apart from everyone and everything.

After the experience of his family leaving, Lincoln kept his windows closed, shut his doors, and remained inside most of the time. In the same manner he sealed off his heart from the rest of the world. He'd installed a telephone downstairs and allowed us to use it, so, I often saw him curled on his long, tan colored sofa, watching episodes of *Dallas* during the week or *Sanford and Son,* on Sunday evening. It was then that we sometimes talked. Whenever I walked in, he looked up and called out to me, "Josette…" having nicknamed me the fiancée of Barnabas Collins from the TV show, *Dark Shadows*. I was a teenager then, extremely self-absorbed, attending high school, and quite pleased with life. Each of my uncles called me by different names; I was happy.

My uncle and I talked about my mother because it was from his apartment that I called her. He told me never to make hasty decisions about my mother's leaving home, that I was too young to understand all the reasons she left, and that one day he was certain I would learn the truth. He seldom ventured into more detail. But I could see he had his own troubles with which to deal. He was alone, isolated and hurting. Out of loneliness, a man does many things. He was already a smoker, a habit that increased with his wife's departure, and on weekends he drank and gambled more often returning home drunk and helpless. Yet, he got up every

Sunday morning and went to church. I found myself wondering exactly what he said to God each Sunday morning after being so out of control just hours before. Images of his swaying body and babbling words about love, life and his pain bewildered me to the extent that I was afraid for him, for what would become of him. Of course, he was outspoken only after drinking. Of course, the following day he could hardly remember what he said. He was like a spoilt egg, no good to anyone. What was worse was that as a little girl I could only imagine my uncle's heartbreak and loss.

As years progressed, my uncle's life took different turns. When Patches died, he was replaced by Ninja, my uncle's need for companionship no longer a secret. Ninja was a dirty brown shabby kind of puppy growing bigger and bigger. Before and after work each day, Lincoln walked and ran with his dog. Seeing him without the rest of his family, I thought that he was as lonesome as his dog. For Christmas, however, my Uncle Lincoln became sociable. He bought gallons of paint, invented colours that he personally mixed; he painted all the walls of our home, outside and inside, in hues of browns, yellows and beiges, toilet and bath included; he tiled the kitchen counter for my grandmother, making our home holiday friendly. He opened his home and entertained family and friends, serving Christmas goodies, alcohol and good cheer. In the years that followed, my Uncle Lincoln came upstairs to my grandmother's twice a day to have breakfast every morning, and for dinner at nights, at which time he gathered scraps of food for his dog, Ninja, his light brown friend and closest companion.

Chapter 7

Michael

My grandmother's youngest son, my Uncle Michael, was a deep thinker and slow talker. He spoke to me in parables. Whenever he saw me sitting alone on the back steps, he'd come up to me, "A riddle, a riddle, who is this little girl? Wha' does she want in life?" or "Girl, what are you thinking about? You mustn't think too much, or else you'll get too smart! And you see what all these smart people in the world doin'!" Michael was tall, the colour of brown sugar. He looked like some kind of guru with long stringy hair that fell on thin shoulders. He had light brown eyes and a long bearded face, which my grandmother always pleaded with him to shave.

Sometimes my Uncle Mike made a lot of money, and other times none. He worked hard installing air-conditioning units and repairing refrigerators. Except for my Aunt Angela, none of my grandmother's children finished high school. Yet, the lessons they taught me cannot be studied inside pages of books or sitting in a classroom. Even if they had the chance to complete school, I think they would have refused, since it would have meant leaving my grandmother, their mother, behind.

I had a special love for my Uncle Mike because apart from being one of my best teachers, he was young, handsome and bright. In my teenage years, I especially enjoyed walking the streets with him, attending school outings in his company, making the young women jealous as we passed along the way. When we walked arm in arm, people often thought he was my boyfriend and kept their distance. At home, my Uncle Daniel always picked on Mike, sometimes because he carelessly sprawled across the furniture with his sweaty feet, at other times because he blasted music from his big silver Sony boom box. Mike didn't argue back. His older brother, my Uncle Daniel, said things you sometimes had to ignore. I begged for Mike, telling Daniel, "You're turning into an old man! Stop quarrelling!"

When I passed the Common Entrance and had to attend Providence Girls' Catholic school for the first time, Uncle Mike took me in a taxi every morning, to show me the route. The first taxi took us from Diego Martin to Port-of-Spain, a thirty-minute ride; another taxi took us from Port-of-Spain to Belmont, another thirty-minute ride. With traffic, the entire trip took about ninety minutes. On busy streets of the capital city, there were no mustard-coloured taxicabs; instead, mini vans called maxi taxis, transported up to thirteen people. There were no skyscrapers except for a few government buildings built only a few years ago. Street vendors and hustlers sold heaps of tamarind, pommeracs, bottled pepper sauce, and stolen rosy mangoes along long and narrow streets. Men sat on the edges of sidewalks, teasing women as they walked by. They sometimes uttered vulgar things about their lips, legs, and breasts, not to mention butt. As I passed them, dressed in my school uniform, I wished I didn't have to become a part of the culture, that I could remain a young girl in Petit Valley, protected under layers of my grandmother's and her children's thick skin. But men looked at me licking their lips, raising eyebrows and sometimes even sticking their tongues out. I wished when I walked the streets to school I could have disappeared, my developing body somehow made invisible under my uniform – or that they'd see me first – a little girl, a person, Sue-Ann. Not my body. Although Mike risked being late for work each day, he accompanied me until I felt comfortable traveling on my own. One day something happened at home that changed things.

I was sixteen, and considered myself responsible. I helped my grandmother with all the chores, went to the market with her every Saturday, and to church with her on Sunday. One Saturday morning I was doing some heavy cleaning around the house, getting rid of unwanted stuff and accumulated garbage. While in Mike's room, I raised his mattress, and decided to dust and remove the stacks of newspapers he had stored under it. *Why did he keep this rubbish*? I piled them neatly with the rest of garbage. Later that day, I went outside and lit a huge fire. Tired, but pleased with my day's work, I sat on the back steps watching the flames rise and bits of ashes fly into the smoke-filled air. That afternoon, when Mike returned home from work, my grandmother was happy to tell him about my cleaning. To our surprise the first thing he asked was, "Where?"

"All about," I butted in. I noticed a tint of worry on his always-cool face. I followed him into his room and heard,

"I realise the place looking clean, I only hope you didn't throw away anything from under my bed!"

"What do you mean, all that garbage you have stored under the bed?" I asked.

He raised the single mattress and saw that all the newspapers had been cleared away.

"What did you do with the papers?"

"Well, I burn them. I lit a big fire and burnt everything!"

"Don't make joke girl!" was the saddened response.

He looked at me, turned slowly, and walked out toward the back stairs into the yard. There he stood with one arm folded, the other, propping his chin. Speechless. He stared at the huge pile of smoking ashes.

"Do <u>you</u> know what you burnt?" he softly managed.

"What?"

"All my savings!"

"Oh my God, I'm sorry, I didn't mean to!" I was astounded!

Silence... hesitation... then

"It gone already, don't worry about it, don't get no horrors," he squeezed out, passing his hand over the top of my head, his long fingers slightly grazing skull. He walked away.

While there was much talk about the incident, and I was scolded over and over by everyone at different times, Mike hardly said another word to me about it. That evening he went to Bobby's, a nearby rum shop, where he drank cold Carib beers until he didn't remember who he was. Alone, I sat on the back stairs, pondering. Alone, I watched Mike as he staggered home. Halfway up the front steps, he stopped to puke. I felt awful. *What a fool I'd been. Why hadn't I checked the newspapers? Why hadn't I known there was money stored in between those sheets of paper?* In the days that followed, I learnt I had burnt over fourteen hundred dollars, his life's savings. In Trinidad, the one hundred-dollar bill had just begun to circulate. It was bright blue with The Coat Of Arms, "Together We Aspire, Together We Achieve" on one side and The Twin Towers (the office of the Prime Minister) on the opposite side. Mike confirmed that from his paycheck he had saved one or sometimes two hundred-dollar bills each week. Using his mattress for a bank, he had carefully stored the crisp blue notes in between sheets of newspapers. This incident became a family joke, though I never thought it funny.

Mike didn't hold me responsible, neither did he make me feel guilty, nor punish me by not talking to me. He seemed to accept the incident as part of his fate, saying things such as "that was how life was; you win some, and lose some." How he went on as if nothing happened still baffles me. He made his usual jokes with me; we spent time together at the movies or at parties, and he spoke to me with the same depth and care he always used. He did not lecture me about making mistakes or about being careful. The experience told me a few things: that money is just paper, the value of which we can determine for ourselves; that my life and experiences are what matter most, and that Mike was the kind of uncle one might see at the movies, the kind of good guy, the star who outlives pain and wrong doing, or he might exist in the deep recesses of a young girl's imagination: the kind of guy any girl would want to know and be loved by. He is my uncle. I've never forgotten that he is as real as the many crisp blue hundred-dollar bills I had mistakenly burnt.

Chapter 8

Daniel

One day, I noticed my Uncle Daniel walking down the back stairs, going towards our back yard. He must have been in his late twenties, medium built, brown-skinned, wearing thick glasses over dark coffee eyes, dressed in white shorts and a white T-shirt with his hairy, muscled legs exposed. I thought he was weeding around the backyard or cleaning the drain, but instead, he suddenly walked up to me, "What are you doing?" he asked, with hands pressed tightly behind his back. Before I could answer, with one swift motion of left hand, he whispered, "Look! I bring a small friend for you. You are looking so lonely sitting under the guava tree!" He stuck a big ugly slimy snail crawling from its hard exterior, and experiencing some discomfort at having been abruptly removed from the dirt, into my face. Seeing the creature's frightening face half out of its shell, I screamed, "Daniel, leave me alone please! Get that thing away from me, please! Tina," I yelled for my grandmother, calling her by first name as I usually did whenever I was in trouble, jumping off the rock upon which I had been sitting, and racing down the rocky slope into our yard. But Daniel was relentless. With snail in his hand, he ran after me up the front stairs, into the gallery, through the living room, into the kitchen, down the back steps, out into the yard again. We made this circuit a few times, me screaming, he persisting, until we were both exhausted or until my Aunt Janet intervened. My grandmother's niece lived in a huge newly built house in front of our home. My Aunt Janet was my grandmother's second sister, Tanty Popo's (her name was Precilla) daughter. She heard my screams, and pleaded with Daniel from their back door. "Daniel! What are you doing the poor girl again?" By that time my cousin Gail and neighbor Keith were both outside watching the scene.

Our concrete houses were built closely together. They were big, high houses with fancy blocks usually painted in white, above wide glass windows. Outside walls were coated in mixtures of flat browns, beiges and whites. Houses had enough space for downstairs extensions with top and bottom back doors peeping into a neighbour's kitchen or living room. Everyday food, fruit, medicine, invitations, and gossip passed over fences from yard to yard. In our neighbourhood, we were all blood relatives, except for three neighbours. What Daniel started off as a joke, always ended up with me screaming desperately, then hysterically crying. Even though I thought it was fun, I sometimes believed my Uncle Daniel was cruel. But over the years, I saw that Daniel was just being the child he never got a chance to be – a mischievous little boy that any parent would have had some measure of difficulty dealing with.

Working at the United Grocers, he started running errands for managers, cutting meat, and packing shelves, moving up over the years, because of his dedication and commitment, to supervisor of the entire stock section. In those days, that was a real accomplishment, especially because my uncle Daniel had not completed school. In a sense, he played the roles of husband, father and big brother, but would not have a wife to complete this scene. He was loved by many women, but never brought any of them home. He didn't spend nights away from home either. At Christmas or on his birthday, he'd return each day from work with bags and sealed packages. During the year, when some of his customers travelled abroad, they brought him bottles of Johnny Walker Black, Blue Nun or sparkling ciders, as a sign of their appreciation for all he did for them. Yet he didn't drink or smoke in our household, Granny, Daniel and I were the only ones who didn't.

Throughout the year, Daniel's bed would often be covered with gift-wrapped boxes of different shapes and sizes tied with satin ribbons, fancy bows, cards and notes neatly stuck in place. I opened them all, and laid out cakes, food items, colognes and aftershave lotions, handkerchiefs, underwear, shirts, socks, and pens, even money, sometimes in USA and Canadian currency! Then I packed them neatly into his drawer. He had his year's supply and enough items to share. The women in his life, customers who frequented the grocery, friends and family members for whom he had done favours, gave him most of these gifts; some were from bosses. Whenever there were food shortages, they all depended on him. When grocery items came in huge truckloads, he kept commodities they needed like potatoes, onions, cheese, and nice slabs of meat. He labelled, packaged, and had items priced and ready for when his customers came grocery shopping. This delighted them, and for this, he was loved more. These were the women to whom he mattered. Some were married, widowed; others were in search of a husband. It made no difference.

There was one fat black lady in particular, Norma, who wanted to marry my Uncle Daniel. Whenever she went to the grocery where he worked she would call loudly, "Dan, Danny Boy, come and sit down here by me, boy! I was looking all over the grocery for you, are you hiding from me?" Then as he tried to sneak past her, she'd grab him, pulling him down into her wide lap, where he would sit, half-embarrassed, his face almost smothered by her oversized sweetly powdered bosom. Norma was married, but she loved him. My Uncle Daniel never gave his heart to anyone. On those occasions, his friends teased him all day long, and when he came home and told us the story, I jeered, "Dan, Danny boy, come and sit down here by me, boy!"

Every week, Uncle Daniel gave my grandmother money she needed to run the house. He kept next to nothing for himself, transportation money, and a few extra dollars. Every time anyone wanted a dollar, they came to Daniel. I still don't know how he managed to have money to give because most times people never repaid him, and he didn't ask. His hobby was handicapping horses. He had a friend who sent him thick red, and also black horseracing books every month from England. Since my eyesight was good, he often asked me to look up names of horses, and special numbers in finely printed pages. Then he re-checked numbers in the black books for details, and spent hours sitting in a warm corner in the gallery, studying every bit of their racing history. He studied their breed and ownership history. How many wins did each horse have? By how many lengths? How long ago? Was there any injury? What kind? He studied jockeys in much the same way, only this time he also included their personal riding habits, skills, and honours, for they, he knew, played an important part. In this way he decided which horse was a good bet, which was better, and which would be the winner. When in doubt, he used his wit combined with knowledge and plain common sense. My Uncle Daniel never gambled family money. Even though he picked winners, he would not bet more than five, or on rare occasions ten dollars. He gave names of prospective winners to family members and friends who often won large sums of money; sometimes they gave him a share of their winnings, many times not. He didn't care. He liked to prove that he could pick a winner!

The more I was in his company, the more I learnt. Uncle Daniel had to assure everyone – especially himself – he was right. That was what he lived for. After all, he'd never had the chance to complete school. This was his way of letting everyone know (especially the smart ones who came to him and wanted to argue about horses, races, and politics) that he was no fool! On the matter of religion, my Uncle Daniel watched my grandmother and me go to church. Whenever relatives and friends gathered at home after mass, he warned "Nearer to church, farther from God." Yet, he willingly gave us money for collection, requesting that we pray for him. It wasn't that he didn't believe in God, it was more that he relied on doing what was right.

As far as politics were concerned, I remember him calling me as a child to watch a man on TV, who'd opposed the government for as long as it had been in power. "Come and see the next Prime Minister of Trinidad and Tobago," he stated as a matter of fact. Indeed, in November 1995, Mr. Basdeo Panday became the first Indian Prime Minister in the history of Trinidad and Tobago, succeeding a government that had run the country for twenty-five years. It was history, and I lived to see my uncle's words come true. I liked to argue politics with Daniel, not because I felt that I was right, but because I wanted to listen to his arguments since I knew he read the daily *Guardian*, Sunday through Sunday. I used to tell him that whoever had great intentions, and seemed capable of running the country would get my vote, that I did not care to which party he belonged, and when that person failed to measure up, I'd change my vote. He admired the way I talked, knowing that much of what I said came from him.

We spent so much time together because Daniel has always been my favourite uncle. We had fun. We jogged together around the Queen's Park Savannah, the largest roundabout in the world. It is about three and a half miles, and is today recorded in the Guinness Book of Records. After jogging, we drank coconut water, and if the green coconuts were still young, enjoyed the soft mushy insides gliding down our parched throats. He told me that because I was skinny, I could eat every thing I liked. As he suffered with back problems, and had been advised by a chiropractor, he was the first to teach me yoga stretches. We did them together on the living room floor. He warned me not to get crazy about dieting. "Just don't overeat!" he insisted.

On any day, extended family members visited our home. My grandmother's consistent weekly menu encouraged these visits. Another alternative to Saturday's menu might be fish broth, a lighter soup with less ground provisions, more fish, the best kind, Red Snapper, or what we call Red fish. It is thoroughly washed in lime, then seasoned with fresh chives (scallions), lots of garlic, herbs and spices. There are no peas and the broth is cooked with carrots, celery, green figs, dumplings, pumpkin and hot pepper. It is good for hangovers and the flu. In the evening, while watching episodes of *Mastana Bahar* showcasing East Indian talent and culture throughout Trinidad and Tobago through song, dance, the sitar and live Indian orchestras, we would have fried king fish and hops bread or bake. On Mondays, we ate leftovers from Sunday's feast of macaroni pie, stewed chicken, rice, beans, *calalloo* (a blend of Dasheen Bush, *ochroes*, pumpkin, seasonings, coconut, and hot pepper). It was my job to make a fresh green salad. Lentil peas, stewed fish or chicken with rice and roti with stewed beans for dinner was her Tuesday menu. On Wednesdays, my grandmother prepared stewed and also curried fish with rice and dhal for lunch, and the same combination for dinner. There was a huge pot of *pelau*, a mix of rice, chicken, pigeon peas, coconut, seasonings and hot pepper every Thursday, and Friday was a no-meat day, so we ate rice with vegetables, or roti with pumpkin and *channa* (chickpeas), *melongene* (egg plant), spinach or bread and New Zealand cheddar. If there was something my grandmother cooked that Daniel didn't like, she simply prepared another dish, covered and left it on the kitchen counter, warning us not to touch it. Still, Uncle Daniel could always muster up a complaint. I saw my grandmother working hard, making trips to the market, washing, cooking, cleaning, and ironing and I heard Daniel complaining.

My tongue was fast. Sometimes when we had company, I talked out of turn. My mouth, the adults said, was as hot as the pepper we ate, and would get me into serious trouble. It was no surprise that at eleven, when I had passed the eleven plus examination for a prestige high school, I believed that I was qualified enough to respond to some of Daniel's complaints. I remember standing beside him when he was at the dinner table. He was about to go into his litany of complaints when I started to rub the middle of his bald-head, and said, "You are starting up again, say sorry, you're just like a bad little child!" He mocked me and replied, "I'm, I'm sorry Tina!" Other times I would say, "What's the matter with you? Can't you simply say, thanks Mummy?" Sometimes if he was in a bad mood, he'd chase me away from the table saying something like, "Miss, I'm not talkin' to you, go, and pick up your schoolbook!"

Uncle Daniel encouraged reading, listening to the news, sports and general issues about knowing more about the country in which I lived, urging me to engage in intelligent conversations. But I think that under the skin of his irritation, he must have been a frightened little boy who complained to cover the loss of a father, and loneliness he felt growing up. After all, *to whom did Daniel complain about such heavy responsibilities of being the head of a household at fourteen? Who cared at all about whether he was tired or frustrated? What about his boyhood days?* I think as time passed I began to make some sense to him because my mother used to tell everyone, "Sue-Ann is the right one to deal with Daniel. She knows him." He looked up to me in a way that he'd not admit, except that I knew he appreciated what I said.

Daniel was also strict. If I didn't complete my homework, was rude to anyone older than I was or if my test results were bad, he'd make me kneel in a corner, facing the wall for many hours, with schoolbook in hand. My grandmother often begged him for me. The whole thing became a joke because he couldn't watch me all the time. So whenever he left to take a nap, my grandmother would bring me snacks, or call me into the kitchen to keep her company where she'd make some of my favorite treats, like sweet rice, or sweet bake. After having eaten my belly full just before he'd reappear, I'd crawl back into the corner, and kneel up straight. When my uncle returned my grandmother would convince him that I had to have dinner! By that time he would have cooled off, and, because he needed me to check horses for him, he didn't mind. Tina and I always believed we had outsmarted him.

Still, Daniel became for me the big brother I needed, and the father presence I never had. I could not remain angry with him for long. When his back hurt, I walked on it. Then I sat on the lower back with my legs spread on either side, and massaged it. He said that whenever I massaged his back, he felt like a line of fine ants were walking on it, and I laughed and told him that was the best I could do. I took that as a challenge. I developed the skill of giving a good back massage. After having not shaved for a couple of days, when the hairs on his face started to grow prickly, he rubbed his beard hard on my cheeks, down my neck. It tickled, it hurt, it made me cry and laugh. We rolled over the bed onto the floor many times. At the beach, I climbed on to his wet shoulders and jumped into the waist-high water sometimes in front, other times behind him, and we'd splash each other's face. Once, a huge wave rolled me over and knocked my bikini top off. Uncle Daniel laughed hard, "Now I could see all your tot tots!" When I think back, I realise how intimate these times were for both of us. He was without a woman; I was without a father. My Uncle Daniel could have forced himself on me many times. He never did. Sometimes, I find myself afraid to be honest about all that Daniel and I shared. I fear I'd be misunderstood. I don't know what it is like for a little girl to have her natural father. But I am certain my relationship with my Uncle Daniel gave me a glimpse of what the experience of having a father might have been like.

Chapter 9

"School Days are Happy, Happy Days"

Miss Roslyn St. Rose was the best looking black woman I'd ever seen. In grade school, at eleven, my 4th standard teacher of average height in her early twenties was of medium build, cocoa powder skin with thick thighs exposed below mini skirts, complemented by psychedelic platforms she comfortably wore. Her teeth glistened under bulging eyes, pleasing to stare into; I suppose because she smiled most of the time. She taught for many years at Petit Valley Girls Roman Catholic School, preparing some thirty something girls every year for eight months to write the Eleven Plus Common Entrance Examination, which upon passing, gained us free access to high school for five years. First class passes guaranteed entry to some of the most prestigious Catholic high schools across the country. Lower grades allowed attendance to government assisted secondary schools; these schools were generally viewed as less competent. Failing students remained in primary school, repeated 4th standard, and only if they had two chances, they repeated the exam one year later. Attendance from 5th standard through 7th followed for students who failed the examination twice.

Miss Piggott, a big strict looking woman with pointed breasts taught older students who didn't pass Common Entrance, but continued from Sixth standard through seventh standard, and those who upon completion of a particular syllabus were awarded a

School Leaving Certificate. Miss Piggott's face almost always looked like a gloomy day. She screamed at students from the top of her lungs, often calling them "stupid". Most everyone was afraid of Miss Piggott, trembling when the angry voice echoed throughout our school. I squeezed my tummy hard whenever I heard her yells. My friends and I never discovered exactly what kind of teacher she was because almost everyone passed Common Entrance Examination, then left primary school before ending up in Miss Piggott's care; we never had the chance to be called "stupid".

In Miss St. Rose's classroom, I sat on the right, second girl behind Rhonda Lewis and Heather Ramsaran, two of my best friends. Later in the term, Miss St. Rose shifted us around, placing slower students on benches nearer to her, a way of keeping sharp eyes on their progress. During the term I was relocated and seated third row towards the back of the class, next to another friend of mine, Kim Ngui (New). We sat closely on wooden benches about one foot wide. From there, without being seen, I could easily pass around red mango, tamarind balls, and chilli-bibi. If caught chewing bubble gum, we had to stand on top of the bench with gum stuck to our foreheads. Most teachers and students who saw us standing there looking foolish, jeered. Nevertheless, our new seating arrangements were perfect. I could pull at Glenda Williams' ribbons, pinch her, and get away unseen. During test, I helped the others with comprehension and vocabulary, while Kim supplied answers to math problems that seemed too complicated to figure out.

Large square board partitions displaying world maps, famous people including the Pope, Queen of England, Prime Minister of Trinidad and Tobago, Dr. Eric Eustace Williams, pictures of beaches, the Taj Mahal and interesting things including tests results decorated our surroundings. Gigantic oblong blackboards separated classrooms. Almost every student from Standard 4A class passed term exams. In term tests, I placed in the first four. My friends and I believed we were Miss St. Rose's favourites, switching spots for first, second, third, and fourth place. For vocabulary, we made a large circle outside the classroom sometimes under shady immortelle trees and royal sky, spelling out words loudly as she randomly called names, reciting synonyms, opposites or words by association. If Miss St. Rose said the word "friend," we could answer "A friend's frown is better than a fool's smile." If she uttered "ambitious," we might add "As ambitious as the devil – as Lady Macbeth." Whenever she turned her back on half the circle, we made funny faces at each other, laughing at those who missed an answer, standing with out stretched hands to receive a ruler that stung already wet palms. Those who flinched, pulling back hands just before ruler contacted skin, received extra lashes.

This was how early education started for us from as young as four and continuing. This is how we memorised verses such as: "As joyful as a fly," and "As lawful as eating." These sayings were recorded in a hard covered orange book called *The Student's Companion*. We each owned a copy. The handy book contained single words, phrases, characteristics, quotations, things about the Queen of Britain, Parliament, small words, big words, comparisons, geographical facts, and general world knowledge. By the time we left Miss St. Rose's class, we had memorised almost the entire book. We used the witty lines not only in day-to-day conversations to boast knowledge, but also to add wit to otherwise dry conversations.

To check homework, especially arithmetic, we formed a straight line towards the side of our teacher's desk. For wrong answers or clear signs of cheating, that is, if several of us used the same method to derive the wrong answer, or vice versa, we got strokes on our calves, which burned terribly, often forming noticeable swellings and discolorations on skinny legs. Anticipating those days, the ones on which our teacher's face told a serious story, and the ones that followed, we wore double socks, futile attempts to brace ourselves from the treacherous sting of the ruler, and jeering from nosy schoolboys.

At lunch time one day, some friends and I planned to rid Miss St. Rose of the ruler; I led the delegation and threw it myself into the ravine that flowed behind the school building, running from the back of St. Anthony's Church. Later, during vocabulary test, when she realised it was missing, a furious Miss St. Rose bolted across classrooms, borrowed two rulers, one from Miss Sutong, the other from Miss Patrick. Miss Sutong was our Second Standard teacher, a Barbie doll, young, fair skinned woman, tiny waist, perfectly made face, and she always wore fashionable clothing with matching scarves and belts. Miss Patrick had bandy legs, wide lips with a decent smile. That afternoon, all I remember was that we were really sorry about the missing ruler. We dared not complain to parents at home because that might have given way to double punishment.

I especially liked rainy days in class because teachers remained in the school kitchen longer, the lunch bell rang later, and then when they returned, the lights were turned off, we got to sing songs, play foot games, or put our heads on desks and sleep. Miss St. Rose conducted after school lessons too, drilled us with comprehension, penmanship, and social studies. Even the slowest learner did well. Our teacher was just that good.

A huge iron bell signalled mid-morning recess. Everyone gathered outside, jamming corridors to get there. Together we lined up in the schoolyard according to class, said a short prayer, one "Our Father" and one "Hail Mary", after which we rattled off with pride our Independence Pledge placing right hands over hearts:

I solemnly pledge to dedicate my life

To the service of my God

And my country.

I will honour my parents

My teachers, my leaders and my elders

And those in authority.

I will be clean and honest in all my thoughts

My words and my deeds.

I will strive in everything I do

To work together with my fellowmen

Of every creed and race

For the greater happiness of all

And the honour and glory of my Country.

We then made eager queues to receive a snack of free milk and sweet biscuits which the government provided. Each of us received one full plastic cup of unsweetened creamy milk, and about six large round milk biscuits. Everyday I prayed that the milk lady would be in a good smiley mood, and give me a few extra biscuits, that being the delicious prize. With cups of milk in hand, we pretended to take gulps, then dashed towards concrete sinks sputtering; we poured the stale tasting liquid down the drain. While some timid girls got beaten up for their biscuits, some of us joined lines for a second time, trying to fool the milk lady.

At lunchtime, we pulled out brown bags. Many of us were so poor that we kept our heads dipped inside greasy paper bags, so that no one could see what little we had. Sometimes, by mistake my grandmother in her morning hurry focusing on her praises to God in song, gave me bread and bread. On such days, I ate the dry sandwich as if there was chicken *chowmein* or New Zealand Cheddar between slices. Whenever my brother Ricky, short for Ricardo, joined my sister Susan and me for lunch, we shared one bottle of Solo (sweet drink), passing it from mouth to mouth, taking in whatever crumbs the other might have left inside the bottle.

Sometimes, Rhonda invited me for lunch at her humble home just minutes away from school on Mojuba Cross Road. Like Rhonda, I was the youngest with one older sister Susan, and one older brother Ricky who also joined us for lunch. Her mother prepared local dishes like rice, dhal and curried *cascadu*, which we wolfed down with glasses of Mauby, washed hands, and scurried back to school giggling, just before the bell sounded. Rhonda's mother Mary was a short petite Indian woman with protruding dark eyes; her father was not usually at home. Whenever he was, we were really quiet; he possessed a strong, strange presence.

When school ended at about 3pm with afternoon prayer, we galloped like happy horses around the schoolyard, screaming, pulling at each other's ribbons, clothing, some older girls playing netball, then scampering out the wide red iron gate to temporary freedom. If we had spare change, we stopped at Miss Cinder's to buy five cents red plums, slices of green mangoes, soaked in hot pepper, salt, lime and garlic. Miss Cinder was a big, fat, black lady who could scarcely fit inside her square red wooden parlor, which was always well stocked. Beads of perspiration rolled down Miss Cinder's face and arms, while she served anxious school children yelling close to her face. We knew that some of her sweat fell into the basin of tamarind stew, whenever she touched her face. We often watched it happen in slow motion. We joked this kept us coming back to her, licking our fingers. Her young daughter resembled her, and had her size, except she was light skinned, and men nicknamed her "Reds". Annette helped her mother, but it was difficult for both of them to move around the small colourful shop, so they often took turns in the morning and afternoon. Both Miss Cinder and her daughter were kind to us, spoke gently, and I thought of them as extra special people. On our way home, we sucked on paradise plums, and tomato balls, candy that cooled burning tongues, but left mouths and lips red, red, red. My sister Susan showed early signs of being a Tomboy. She usually went home with a group of boys from the Boys' School on the opposite side of the street, together with my brother Ricky. They took shortcuts, hung out in the river or rode bikes home.

My daily allowance was twenty-five cents, ten cents for bus fare both ways, and five cents pocket change. Walking to and from school gave me more pocket money. If I walked home with Kim, and her three sisters, Hazel, June and Moi, I would get there in about twenty minutes moving with their agility and speed. Kim and her sisters did not have many friends or pocket change. In fact, they mostly kept to themselves, but because I talked my way into their lives, I got a close up view.

My friends were Chinese girls with bangs and long ponytails that swung in time with the pace they kept. There were four of them neatly dressed walking in single file, with me trying to catch their pace, steps behind. Halfway between school and home, on Morne Coco Road, just before Hibiscus Drive, Kim and her sisters dashed into an odd looking house hidden behind overgrown shrubs and crotons. I played near a standpipe chasing butterflies on bright yellow buttercups, basking under the silvery morning sun. My three friends quickly emerged from the house securing what seemed like small lunch bags between schoolbooks. Every day they came out with the same expressionless faces, said nothing and I didn't ask a question. We continued to school without talking.

In all the years that Kim and I knew each other, from the age of five when we started primary school, and later when we both attended the same high school, I met her parents only once, and visited her home just once or twice. In all, Kim had 10 siblings, her mother, a small frail woman named Dorothy, and her father Bertrand, completing a family of thirteen. Survival for Kim and her family must have been even more difficult than I could have imagined.

At the end of school terms we eagerly looked forward to school trips. Our class visited the Coca Cola/Cannings Factory,

Nestle's Factory, and Brechen Castle Sugar Factory. Preparing for these trips was fun, figuring what to wear, how to comb hair without ribbons, picking out lunch and snacks. Long bus rides promised excitement. Country landscapes energised us sitting, next to best friends, singing songs, playing word games, giving jokes, while lightly teasing each other. I always took notes, knowing that on our return Miss St. Rose would give essays to write. Of all our school trips, the one to the sugar factory was most interesting. Seeing stacks of muddy cane piled some twenty feet into the air, hauled into big wheel barrows and transported to the gigantic factory where they'd pass through various grinding, cleaning, milling machines finally emerging into shiny brown crystals was simply the most amazing. The history of sugar cane fields in Trinidad is linked to our indentured labour history, and to the presence of East Indians, they, having been transported from India from as early as 1845 to work in these fields located in Central Trinidad, preparing land for cane farming. The East Indians prepared the land, planted, tended, cut and hauled cane. East Indians of Trinidad and Tobago created their own history, contributing to the rich ethnic blend of culture present in Trinidad and Tobago, past and post colonisation.

Ann Simon was a black girl who wasn't particularly pretty, but you were forced to give her a second glance because she was fierce looking. She was one of Petit Valley Girls' school bullies; her older sister Margaret was another. One day, while standing in line under the blazing sun, Ann Simon pulled lice that had been crawling between long braided ribbons, pranced to the top of the line pressing the miniature creatures between thumb and index fingers, screaming "Ah ha, Sue-Ann has lice, Ah ha, Sue-Ann has lice!" Turning in shame, rubbing watery eyes, I told her to mind her own business, that I got it from Heather, who got it from Rhonda, who got it from somebody else. I was more than embarrassed. Ann also had the habit of snatching things from me and running off. I took this treatment from her for a long time, until one day I decided I had had enough. Another time, when Ann

Simon made a big commotion singing, "*Coolie, Coolie come for roti, all the roti done, mash potato, mash potato, all the roti done!*" Embarrassed, I lowered my head, then suddenly like a waiting tiger sprinted into her face and shouted, "Picky head *nigger* rice and *channa*."

Ann Simon's black face changed colours; it immediately took the dark shade of *melongene*. She was so humiliated that she ran after me over and over through the schoolyard, with her hand in a fist. But when she couldn't catch me, she eventually gave up. For many days following the incident, she left me alone, staring at me from the corners of her eyes. I walked home from school with Kim and quickly got to safety. It was the first time that anyone had called Ann "*nigger*," just as it was also the first time that someone had called me "*coolie*." I wasn't even sure what it all meant. That being said, Ann and I had looked each other deep in the eye; it was a long hard silent look that sharply penetrated our skins.

Weeks later, while at school one day, I approached Ann and asked if I could play with her Barbie. She brought Barbie, other dolls, and toys to school, hidden in a fancy schoolbag her mother sent from America. Funny how that day she let me play with her Barbie, and I shared a piece of *belly-full* with her. In a cool spot near the back gate close to bushes, we sat and played with Barbie; Ann brushed my hair over and over, plaiting and unplaiting strands to suit herself. We chatted, giggled, and got to know each other a little better. Many curious girls walked by peeping at Ann and me, feeling frightened for me, waving me to move away from Ann, wondering since when we played together. But I did not listen. After that afternoon Ann Simon and I were inseparable.

As friends, if I walked with Ann after school, with Kim and her sisters out of sight, well I got home much later, as this new routine turned into stealing adventures. Ann and I stole rosy *pommeracs*, and various fruit from some foreign white man whose name we never knew, and who owned property on Morne Coco Road. He had an estate of king oranges, *pommeracs*, sapodillas, coconuts, and mangoes. The main obstacle was that while his fence faced the roadside, in order to get to the *pommerac* tree, we had to run down a long concrete path in front of the stranger's house past where the fence started, then up a good few hundred yards towards the road where various fruit trees dropped mouth watering ripe fruit. Our job was to fill school bags; pockets and skirts, then scamper out of the area. Sometimes we would become so distracted we'd sit under the *pommerac* tree for hours eating fruit, rolling on the ground, and filling our bellies.

It was rumoured that the owner had a shotgun and wasn't afraid to use it if he had the chance. What a pair Ann Simon and I became. Ann liked the fact whenever we had to, I proved myself to be just as fast as she was. A few times we heard "Get out! Get out!" and then a loud bang. Ann and I ran for our lives out of the stranger's yard, passing Casalle's corner, straight down Morne Coco Road. I even ran past my stop at Crystal Stream Avenue, dropping Ann off at her corner, Simeon Road. When we eventually stopped running, we could hardly recognise each other: watery eyes, trembling bodies, falling socks and untidy uniforms, ruffled hair with half tied ribbons. On several occasions, I went up Simeon Road to Ann's home. Although it was a tough hill to climb, panting as I climbed, yet, I remembered the breathtaking view of the Valley below, wondrous mountains, simply majestic. We were so scared that we never set foot in that white man's yard again. Ann and I discovered other fruit trees to raid, and even though we leaped from bad dogs, jumped walls, hit guava, hog plum, and *mango calabash* trees, this was done under far less threatening circumstances. Still, Ann and I lavished in each other's company, and most of all, the feeling of excitement, adventure, and escape we both unleashed.

I never worried about passing Common Entrance because Miss St. Rose always assured us we were doing great. But one of my grandmother's older sisters, Tanty Popo had a plan B for me. She had Shango Baptist friends who lived in San Juan, and who she often visited. Tanty Popo invited my grandmother and me for what is still called "Thanksgiving Feast." It is a celebration of prayer, sacrifice and sharing. I never knew any of the Baptist ladies' names, except that everyone referred to them as Mother and Sister. Months before the eleven plus examination, when we visited for the ceremony, my grandmother asked me to write the names of schools I wanted to attend, as well as the names of friends I wanted to pray for. I made a long list asking God to please make sure all my friends and I, passed for the same school.

At the altar on the day of the ceremony, I placed the list into a jar together with many other requests and petitions. I suppose those were also prayer requests. The altar was huge and colourful, decorated with lace, Christian statues and saints, crosses, fruits, water, bells, some things I easily recognised, others I did not. Asking questions was of course a no, no. After prayer, worship, chants, songs and invocations we all shared in a lavish meal of blessed food, fruit and drink, taking along bags of goodies to share with friends and family. Mother was a serious looking dark skinned woman. In the beginning, I was afraid of her, but after a few visits to their home, whenever she put her hand on my shoulder and whispered, "Don't worry child, everything will be alright," I not only believed her, but also trusted her guidance. Months later when two of my best friends, Heather, and Kim, and I actually passed for the same high school I had personally petitioned to God, Providence Girls', I looked up to the heavens, and said my own special "Thank You God." I developed a new respect for Shango Baptist people.

Chapter 10

Susan and Ricardo

It will soon be my sister's birthday, April 7. I don't remember sharing many birthdays with her. Apart from being the eldest, she is also my only sister. I am the youngest. Susan is the kind of person who goes out of her way to please people; she thinks she always has to prove herself. My sister came to the USA on my stepfather's suggestion in 1986, just after our wedding. He said maybe new surroundings will give her a new zest for life. Even though she was an Accounts Clerk in Trinidad earning a good salary, she knew by coming to the USA without resident papers, the only alternative might be for her to obtain a babysitting job, in the hope her employers would sponsor her for a Green Card. While my sister loved children, and like me also had experience caring for my Aunt Angela's six, she also decided from an early age she would never have any of her own, a promise she made to herself. The pain of sex, my sister often explained, the weight of pregnancy, the torture of delivery, and the round the clock care the infant needed after birth seemed overwhelming. She had witnessed first-hand many joys and endless challenges involved in having and raising children and especially the effort required in keeping a family together, my sister managed to zero in on the pain.

Susan settled in the USA. Not long afterward, a friend of a friend got her the first babysitting job. During the week, she worked for a Jewish family somewhere in New Jersey, travelling on weekends to Aunt Theresa's home in Brooklyn. This experience was short lived for her because apart from being a babysitter, the family insisted she also become their maid with meagre pay, high expectancy, and bad treatment. My sister held the job for as long as she could, before finding another one. This time her employers were a middle class white American family who lived on Staten Island. There she found a home within a home and remained employed with the Feinbergs for several years. My sister instantly developed a good relationship with her employers, but whenever there was the usual trouble expected in most marriages, my sister started to internalise such events, as if they were her own fault. Whenever I listened to some of her accounts and while I also felt saddened, I realised people were responsible for their own lives. On the contrary, that realisation became more of a challenge for my sister. She started to assume some kind of internal blame. Consequently, when the couple decided after years of fighting with each other to divorce, my sister took it personally and immediately started job hunting, concluding she couldn't cope with their break-up.

In many ways, I suppose my sister was still living in the past, remembering when a happy family, her own, broke up, and how she felt handling the pain of the break-up. I suppose as well she internalised the whole story of her employers, to the point where she must have somehow started believing she was the cause of the split between husband and wife, even though she obviously was not. I started piecing my sister's fragile life together without her knowledge. Maybe she even blamed herself for our parents' broken marriage. I could not have known how the experience of watching her mother leave home, then later her father's leaving impacted her life. I had a vague recollection of her reaction to what was going on around our family.

Like my mother, my sister Susan was born under the fiery sign of Aries. We were opposites from the beginning. I believed the sun, moon, and stars had some effect on our lives, and early on, when my best friend Felicia introduced me to Sydney Omar, the astrology prince, I was convinced the stars played some part in linking our behaviour to who we were on planet Earth. Born under Saturn, ruler of Capricorn, Felicia and I connected our similarities, shared our likes and dislikes, and like two young girls charted our paths in life. We often thought the same thoughts, laughed at the same jokes, and on several occasions came out dressed in the same colors. How else could we have explained such universal connectedness? From early, my friend and I decided we were different *only* by skin colour and upbringing. From the start, we knew in the eyes of God these things didn't matter.

Throughout school life, my sister Susan indicated how different she was: she loved to ride bikes, and was often caught with boys riding long distances on busy streets, returning home later with bruised knees and bloody elbows. She usually went with a group of boys from the Boys' Catholic school across the street hanging out, taking short cuts, and acting as if she was one of them. Whenever my mother sent us gifts such as cotton dresses, skirts and delicate underwear, my sister openly expressed her disappointment. Susan usually specifically requested jeans and tees.

In Trinidad, my sister attended a private high school that was the first of its kind, gaining an occupational education. This meant apart from academics, every young girl graduated with skills, and also job training. Corpus Christi College of Occupational Education and Training was an all-girl Catholic school run by Carmelite sisters, dressed in dark brown overalls, and long thick veils that covered most of their faces. The nuns were strict and scary looking. My sister enjoyed life at school, busying herself with school activities, cake sales, car washes, weekend retreats, and job fairs. Most important to her was spending time with her friends. To me that was her real joy. Her girlfriends visited our home, eating whatever my grandmother had to offer, each one trying to be liked the most, asking my grandmother who was her favorite. My grandmother cunningly convinced them they all were, secretly winking her eyes at each of them. While I liked many of my sister's friends at first meeting, there were one or two that I did not. Actually, when I heard them declare I was a snob, I made every effort to keep my distance.

It was during her teenage years that my sister started showing clear signs of rebellion. Being two years younger than she was, I didn't go everywhere she went; in fact, she didn't want me following her. She feared I might report to Granny her comings and goings, report what I heard and all their plans. My sister went to parties, drank herself silly, and started smoking cigarettes. It wasn't the first time she smoked cigarettes, because I had heard after school she went with some of the boys, walking towards the river where they puffed cigarettes. My grandmother was fast becoming worried, warning Susan with finger pointed towards her face, "Be careful of the company you keep, friends will lead you astray, but they won't be there to bring you back." But my sister paid little attention to these warnings, often having quarrels at home, making disagreements the excuse to storm out the house, so she could hang out with friends. Always, my sister put her friends first, leaving us behind to worry about when she would return home or whether or not she was safe. My grandmother seldom shut her eyes whenever Susan was out late at night, tossing and turning until the moment she heard the squeaking front door open. Only then would my grandmother turn towards me grabbing for the cotton coverlet, hug me closely, and fall asleep.

After a lovely high school graduation at which many local government officials were present including Sir Ellis Clarke, the previous President of Trinidad and Tobago, who played a major role in obtaining government subsidies to the school, my sister, together with all her classmates became permanently employed. They were the first group of girls to graduate under the occupational title. This served as a positive example, since private companies also invested heavily in the school, as they were assured "fine young women" who were not only academically qualified, but were also skilled, trained, and willing to start at the bottom of the corporate ladder, and work their way to the top.

At first, after graduation, my sister settled nicely into the job, only months later to become restless. She soon started changing jobs quickly; she began taking too many days off, not being consistent, and wanted to run off on vacation whenever she pleased. My aunts were becoming worried. They spoke to my mother about their eldest niece. My sister, Susan, and my stepfather discussed the matter. They quickly made a decision. It was decided my sister would leave Trinidad to settle in Tobago with my mother and stepfather. On hearing the news, my sister was openly angry. She stormed out of the house and spent several days and nights hanging out with the friends without checking in at home. I found myself thinking *how could my mother take her away from us, and also from the only life she knew? What kind of life was she, a young woman, expected to live in Tobago? Tobago was quiet, boring for many.*

Susan moved to Tobago, and attended St. Joseph's Convent. As expected, she had difficulty settling down, always inviting friends from Trinidad to spend weekends at my mother's home, especially whenever family was away. It wasn't long before my mother and stepfather decided Susan might need professional help, she might even need to see a psychiatrist – that there might be things going on in her head she had not been disclosing to anyone – that her behaviour was not usual, and that over time it may have been worsening. My mother made appointments for Susan to visit with one Dr. Ghany whose office was located in Trinidad. Reluctantly, Susan started these visits, using some of the time in Trinidad to hang out. Over a period of months, Dr. Ghany related to my mother some of his medical findings regarding my sister and her irresponsible behaviour. Dr. Ghany told my mother that my sister had developed a deep resentment for her – that she blamed her for walking out on our father and family. She felt responsible for our parents break-up, and in her mind my sister felt burdened by the responsibility of having a younger brother and sister to look after. Dr. Ghany informed my mother my sister was extremely talented and intelligent; she was also capable of building stories to fit into her own fantasies about what she wanted in life – about what was real or not. Obviously when reports about Susan and Dr. Ghany reached family members, every one grew concerned, most especially our Aunt Angela.

After trying to develop a closer relationship with Susan based on Dr. Ghany's reports, my mother eventually disclosed to her some of the doctor's findings. My sister adamantly refused to continue seeing the doctor, saying because he had betrayed her confidentiality, he could not be trusted. My sister's irresponsible behaviour continued to spiral downhill. Many of her friends could no longer help her, and even though they became worried, they also had their own lives.

Susan moved between Trinidad and Tobago whenever she wanted, having no real sense of purpose in life, no balance, no desire to achieve anything. It was around 1984 when my stepfather first suggested to my mother, to send my sister away to America. He said maybe a different place would be good for her, with new surroundings, he suggested maybe she'll find her own way. My mother agreed, and quite surprisingly to everyone when she was told, so did my sister. By that time I was already dating a young man, Anthony for two years. The thought of my sister leaving for America was hard to accept. *Where was she going? Where would she live? Who would take care of her?* My sister convinced me not to worry. When the time came around, she believed things would work out. I saw in her eyes she believed in this new chance – that she wanted the adventure of moving somewhere unknown.

My boyfriend and I were engaged in 1985, and started planning a wedding for September 1986, while at the same time my sister had also decided to leave for America immediately after our wedding. My sister promised to be there for me at our wedding as my chief bridesmaid. No matter what, whenever my sister pledged to be there for someone, she usually made it happen. You could depend on her. Being her little sister, I trusted her word. Unfortunately, my stepfather didn't live to see either my sister leave for America or me get married. Susan was beginning to see his truth. My stepfather's death deeply impacted her life. From the moment following our stepfather's death and burial, a transformed Susan was present with me every step of the way; she shared the dream of my wedding and future happiness. Our relationship grew stronger during that period, the time of my wedding, and also her leaving for the USA. Our dependency on each other for support and love was visible to everyone. It would be one of the last things she, my only sister, did for me before leaving home for America. It was one of the best impressions of my sister.

My sister spread warmth wherever she went. Susan needed to be needed, wanted to be loved. It seemed to me she carved a life around those needs. She was a loving, gentle person gaining trust in an instant, and being betrayed by friendship and love time and time again. She was the clinging kind of person who would place the world at your feet, once she had it to give. She almost always stifled her feelings, hiding what she wanted to say, giving way to people's demands. In 1986, just after our wedding, my sister Susan left our humble home in Trinidad and travelled to the great land of America hoping to find anything she might be searching for her whole life.

Conversations with my sister became strained, mostly ending in arguments. She compared herself to my far from perfect life: my marriage, job, son, always going after the things I wanted is what she intimated to me – always strong, focused. Bette Midler's "Wind Beneath My Wings" was how my sister often thought of me. This is how my sister still sees her little sister. With all my day-to-day struggles, I somehow managed to continue moving forward, with disappointments, setbacks, lost loves, no money, I still go on. How? As I try to make more sense of my sister's life, and my own, I understand how different our roads have been – how difficult it must have been for Susan to see my mother walk out on our family, and know she wasn't coming back – to blame herself – to be present when my father also walked away from our grandmother's home – and the agony of what it must have felt for her being the older sibling. In many ways, I know my sister and I have walked similar paths of solitude.

I

My brother Ricardo Gregory was given a second chance at life from very young. At five, a truck knocked him off the side of the street where he had been walking. He suffered massive brain damage, lost use of his right hand, and spent more than six months in Port-of-Spain General Hospital. Doctors confirmed he was lucky to have survived, given the acute damages to his head. As a result, he never completed primary school, and for most of his life, he was cushioned by everyone into maturity.

Over time, because of his irrational behaviour, people believed he was half crazy, but gave way to him. It seemed he was fine, but then quite unexpectedly he would burst into fits of anger. On one such occasion, he chased me around the house with a lighted starlight, the sticks that come in a box. When I tried to escape his pursuit by running upstairs to my grandmother, he pounced near me from behind, pressing the flame to the spot behind my left knee. The moment I yelled out in shock and pain, he scurried away laughing; I couldn't walk for days. The burn left a nasty scar behind my left knee, which my grandmother nursed for weeks. On another occasion, he was towing me on his bicycle, when I slipped off, he dragged me for yards with me in tears begging him to stop. Whenever incidents similar to these occurred, I was convinced he was a bit crazy.

He didn't live very long with us at my grandmother's home in Petit Valley either. Perhaps it was for the same reason of his lack of control for his actions. He soon left Trinidad to live in Tobago with my mother and stepfather. Ricardo attended Scarborough Anglican School only until Seventh Standard; that was all the formal learning he could take; he was about fifteen. I saw him only when I visited, and in my stepfather's presence he seemed quite subdued. But my mother spoilt him rotten, maybe even blaming herself for his accident. He got everything he wanted, her way of making up for the mistake of his accident.

My brother loved music, from early on he had his music set up, complete with large boxes, and before CDS, he collected songs that have long been forgotten on cassettes. He became a DJ, building his own little world around himself and his music. He remembered people and places, and was quite likeable. Born in November, a Scorpio, he was like salt fish in the centre of people's lives; but he was genuine. He gave from his heart without expecting anything in return. Much unlike me, my brother didn't have to get to know someone for years; once he met you, he liked you, especially if you were one of our friends. He remained with a child like innocence all through his adult life, something I have admired in him for as long as I have known him. You had to be up close and personal to notice something was wrong. But you had no choice, but to love him once you got a clear picture of how he survived.

One day my brother met one of my sister's coworker's little sister and his life took a different turn. The first time he saw her he fell in love with Indie, and cared for her in a way that sometimes surprised me. My brother travelled more often to Trinidad to spend time with the girl. Even though she lived in San Fernando, South of Port-of-Spain, the distance meant nothing to him. He travelled by public transportation there to see her; he was liked by her family. For years, he bought her expensive jewellery, gave her the best of what he had to offer, and put her before himself. Eventually they married. Sadly, the union was short-lived as we later learnt that Indie used my brother Ricky to escape the strong ties of her family. *Perhaps she was too young for marriage. Maybe she didn't love my brother. Maybe she wanted a reason to break her family ties*, I found myself thinking over and over. *But why him? Why did she have to choose him?* They dated for more than seven years. Couldn't she have said no? My brother was vulnerable and I suppose that made him her prey. With him still living in Tobago, and she in Trinidad, she soon started seeing an older married man, who had a family of his own. Whenever my brother and his new wife met in Trinidad, she was different, and had drastically changed.

My mother discovered through Indie's sister what had happened, sadly only after a few months their marriage ended. Indie's family apologised, and remained close to my brother because they loved him. It was a tough wound for my brother to bear alone. I felt sorry for him and his loss, I wanted to be there for him for the rest of his life. I didn't know whether he had it in him to survive the heartbreak. He didn't eat for days, barely came out of his room. But he turned to his music to pass his days. With time, he has become a stronger person, leaving his past somewhere behind, but occasionally remembering the pain.

My relationship with both my sister and brother has mostly been one of acceptance. When you realise early in life you cannot change some circumstances of your life, you quite painstakingly learn to accept what was handed to you. I believe it has been one of my survival tools. With every new experience we share, we have grown. My brother and I became closer mostly because we are family. In many ways, we both understand this and make the effort to leave the past right where it belongs. Time spent with each other is less strained. We recently learned through scans and x-rays that my brother's right brain never grew; it remained the size of a child's. He was lucky to have lived a full life, despite this physical disability. I appreciate him even more. Both my siblings and I are in our forties, and although we still live different lives, are constantly drawn together in love by this precious thing called our DNA.

Chapter 11

Life, Love and Death at 18

My life has been a series of beginnings and failings, of starting over. My parents separated when I was only two; I lost my first love when I was almost eighteen. We were both just out of high school. My boyfriend was pinned down by the same tractor he had been driving on the north coast of our island. He was small, handsome, and bright with sparkly light brown eyes. To make himself feel important, he talked a lot, made up his own jokes to make me laugh, and was, I thought, much too grown for his age. I didn't care. I never believed there was something in life that could tear away at me: death, I quickly learnt, could.

He wasn't the first boy to press hot lips against mine. But some twenty-five years later, his were the ones I could still taste. His lips reminded me of the ocean's spray, surprising, playful; just like the ocean, deep. His hands owned my body, and I let them. Dexter Anthony Pillai came into my life for the first time when I was in Form 4, one year before high school graduation; I was not yet 17. Our class trip for Easter weekend took us to Monos Island. A group of excited young girls, two teachers, with bags filled with goodies piled into a 20 foot boat that left from Chaguaramas to the deserted island. We carried fancy bikinis; hot denim shorts and tees, and were all anxious to hang out late, listen to scary stories, and bond with girlfriends over delightful meals.

By the time we got to the island, and started offloading our stuff we realised we were the only ones on the deserted island for the weekend. This revelation delighted us even more. While some expressed fear, our teachers assured us there was nothing to be scared about. She reminded us being surrounded by nature was a good thing; we were safe. Settling in, we shared rooms, and while unpacking, flaunted our skinny bodies, singing disco songs and dancing about the place. We joined the others to help prepare dinner. It was near dinnertime, when we were distracted by loud laughter and noise coming from the jetty area, only a couple hundred yards away from the house. A few of us immediately ventured down. We discovered some more students had arrived for the weekend; they came from another high school, St. James Secondary. Unlike our group, this one included boys. At first we were visibly upset, and even showed signs of our unwillingness to share the island, but with a few quick introductions, we realised not only did we not have a choice in the matter, but what sense did it make to remain upset when we were supposed to be having a fun-filled weekend. I quickly convinced my friends we could still have a great time.

In the group we met at the jetty, there were two boys who came forward as leaders, the first was Dexter, and the second we came to know as his best friend Twitz. My girlfriends immediately commented how cute they thought Dexter was, and asked my opinion. I said he was OK and I didn't think much of him since first impressions were lasting ones, and he seemed to have already made his. For one thing, he talked too much, and secondly, he seemed self absorbed. In the few minutes we all met, he was the one doing most of the talking, with others randomly chiming in. I decided early I was going to keep out of their way, not let their presence on the island ruin our weekend.

After our brief encounter that night, we returned to the weekend house and had hot dogs for dinner. We washed up, and got ready for bed. Charlotte then decided she wanted to go for a moonlight walk. We couldn't let her go out alone, and so a few of us dressed in homemade cotton pajamas, accompanied her through the narrow path down to the jetty, brushing past green shrubs and smelly bushes. The sky was moonless. By the time we got to the far end of the jetty, we noticed there was a group of people gathered there. We discovered our neighbours hanging out on the jetty, and we were invited to join them. Besides their boom box blasting 70s disco, they were telling scary stories, sitting snugly next to each other, and laughing. I grew uncomfortable and when I gestured to return to the house, was out voted. Dexter was talking loudly, standing up, gaining everyone's attention. He wasn't a big guy, but there was something captivating about his demeanour. Edging up in a corner closer to Charlotte, I could not help but notice how everyone looked up to him; he was the centre of attention. Everything he said made sense, he was funny, and yes I eventually admitted only to myself, he was also good-looking. He suddenly drew his attention to me, throwing random questions my way. I didn't answer or give information about my life. This bothered him, and then just like that, I became the subject of his jokes. He commented about my long hair being too long, and how bony I was. By the time we were ready to leave the jetty, my wandering mind determined he was big fool.

It seemed the next day, Dexter and I were on the island alone because everywhere I walked he was present. At lunchtime he was close by bringing me some of their cooking to taste. The moment I stepped into the icy water, he was also within range playing soccer on the sand, occasionally exhibiting his swimming skills by diving into the water to retrieve the ball, splashing water into my face, apologising, and then running off. My friends told me he liked me, and said he felt badly for embarrassing me the night before. They said he was trying to make amends. I didn't believe them. To me, he was craving attention. Later that night, we had a party, and decided to include our new friends. Although Dexter and I did not have a conversation that night, he danced within arms length, stood close by; several times during the night our eyes made curious fours.

The following day, Sunday, their group planned to leave early; we gathered at the jetty to say goodbye. I watched as they all piled into the boat, when Dexter put on a funny performance. As the boat roared off, he removed his T-shirt, dove into the water, swimming a few yards to the jetty where he reached up, and carved his phone number with a small pocket knife upon the wooden floor; he demanded I call him. Everyone was hysterically laughing, and teasing me. Besides being embarrassed by him for about three times that weekend, I was convinced he was a show off. I decided I would not call him; I did not write down his number.

The weekend events subsided; we returned to school the following week, having put the experience down in our memories as a great weekend; my friends constantly taunting me to call the boy. My excuse was I didn't have his number, but of course my friend Charlotte, had memorised it. Besides, she reminded me we could get it from the phone directory, since he carried a name we could not forget, Pillai as in Pillai's Hardware, Pillai's Gas Station, and Pillai's Autoparts.

A couple of weeks passed. Sometimes secretly I wondered about Dexter, and some of the things he shared with us on Monos. He said he was Pisces born. *I wondered whether he was all we saw that weekend or whether what we saw was really his exterior covering up his inner self, the real person. I even believed he might not have a happy life, and so had to make up for whatever he lacked whenever he went out in public. My last thought was no wonder he could swim being born under the sign of fish.*

One morning at school, an excited Charlotte came by. She told me she had something for me. She mentioned she met Dexter, since they lived on almost the same route. That morning he excitedly stopped the truck he had been driving, hurriedly ran towards her, quickly questioning her about me, whether or not I had a boyfriend, whether I said if I liked him, whether I might go out with him. She said she told him I didn't have a boyfriend, and I would go out with him. Charlotte told me then and there she liked him for me, and gave me his phone number which was scribbled on a piece of paper, in the same way it was carved on the wooden floor at the jetty on Monos Island. She said he begged her to get me to call him. Charlotte was certain Dexter loved me. I believed Dexter was extremely bold, but brave as well. I called him.

Dexter and I went out on a few dates, but he decided we were not dating. He visited me at home, picked me up, he didn't make any romantic moves toward me, and we became friends. I learnt he was from an affluent family who had businesses; the surname he carried was well respected. Time passed, and I figured that was all there was to our friendship. But one afternoon when I walked to the corner of Belmont Circular Road, and Dexter picked me up in his uncle's white and black Ford with a souped up V-6 engine, and sunroof, everything changed. I knew about the car because he had boasted about driving it when we were on Monos. Although the car belonged to his Uncle Steve, he referred to it as his favourite girl. From all he said, it was clear he loved it to the point of obsession. Getting into the car, I noticed his hair was dripping wet, and he smelt expensive; it was mesmerising. When I asked him whether he poured the bottle of cologne over himself, he jokingly replied it was "imported stuff, Paco Rabanne." The boy was smooth. Just ten minutes away, he made a right turn at Belmont Circular Road,and drove me to his grandmother's place in Maraval, a huge upstairs home located above the family's hardware store.

Still dressed in school clothes, Dexter led me towards the entrance, up a long concrete staircase. I didn't see his grandmother, because he said she was asleep in her room, and he mentioned her door was usually kept shut. He told me I would have the chance to meet her another time. At the top of the stairs there was a parrot just sitting in his cage watching things. Dexter told me to be quiet since I might wake him and then he'd cause a ruckus. I told him the parrot was already awake and looking at me with bright, beady eyes. He smiled. I did as I was told. Dexter opened the door to a well-furnished room, and waved me in. I stumbled in, gazed around, trying to seem relaxed. I wasn't. We sat near the edge of his uncle's bed. It was a large beautifully made bed, sheets embroidered with red and pink bunches of roses. Dexter told me I could take off my socks and sneakers, and I did. He told me ever since our meeting on Monos Island, he could not steady his mind; he had to see me alone. Dexter sat close to me; he put his arm around me, and immediately started undressing me. First he pulled the crisp white blouse out of my skirt, carefully unbuttoning each button. I felt his fingers not upon my bare back, but over my vest, bra and skin; his fingers tickled my body forcing me to my feet. He stood beside me, removed my vest over my head, unhooked my bra, unzipped my skirt letting it fall, slip, and then panties. With his hands he raised each leg so I slid out of the clothing lying at my feet. He didn't fumble, wasn't afraid, and in an instant I knew he had some idea of what he was doing. I never said No. I was naked before him. Realising this, and in embarrassment I held both hands over my breasts; smiling, he grasped both hands pressing them upon his cheeks, "No you don't."

Dexter watched me with such intensity, I could never forget, my nervous face, twitching body; he unplaited my braids, tracing his warm fingers along my spine. Then I felt his tongue fall upon my back, stroking me in gentle upward movements. I had never been touched this way. He sat behind me, taking off his T-shirt, pulling me down over his body, his hands grasping both breasts. I turned towards him, and removed his pants and jockeys. One glimpse of his hardened penis frightened and aroused me at the same time; I wanted this young man. He was fine boned and sexy. Without wasting time, our bodies became entwined in the same rhythmic dance, the same hungry breath.

My mind drifted in and out to earlier that day at school, I remembered the day, how lovely it was; the sky had been a brilliant blue with small clouds just like sail boats. School went well especially because my friend Elizabeth gave me news that she had seen Dexter on her way home the day before, and he gave her the message he wanted to see me after school – he would pick me up at the corner of Belmont Circular Road, when I was on my way home – I should not worry he would take me home. Even though my friends teased me all day, I tried not to show it; but privately I just couldn't wait for the end of day to meet with Dexter, the person whose ways I was now curious to learn about. So I spent the day mostly daydreaming in class, thinking about what would happen when Dexter and I met later that day, and I focused on how much I wanted to taste his lips, mouth to mouth. He kissed me before, but it was always a "Hello, glad to see you kind of kiss," or "Goodnight, see you tomorrow." And in the middle of all those thoughts about kisses, I felt a sudden sharpness – a steady thrust – pain; tears streaming down tightly shut eyes – thrusting – pain, and a quiet sweetness I had not known in this pain – kisses, caresses, touches, soft movements mingled with steady pushing, swaying hips, and hard panting. As much as I tried to stifle screams, while being swallowed by his mouth covering my mouth, sounds came bursting through. "Sssh…" Dexter whispered. His grandmother's bedroom was only footsteps away. He was inside me, holding me down, gripping hands, kissing eyes, lips, grabbing my hips. His tiger-eye eyes shone glassy and beautiful; in that moment, I willingly surrendered to his loving me. We looked deep into each other's eyes, and without understanding many things about life and our meeting, also understood many things. This seventeen year old young man became my world; in this world we lived for each other. I got to know Dexter in the same intimate way I learnt about his favourite scent.

When our first love making session ended, there were sheets to be washed, a soiled mattress to be scrubbed, and I worried. Dexter put it all in a neat bundle on the floor assuring me there was nothing to worry about. He was more concerned about how I felt. After a warm shower in which he joined me, and washed my body from head to toe, we had ice cream, and soft caresses. He drove me home that evening with me sitting so closely to him, he could barely change gears. By the time I got home I started to doubt he was a fool, thinking instead he was a man.

In the following months, I came to know a love as gentle as a soothing breeze, under an afternoon's sunset. Dexter came to our school bazaar; arm in arm we skipped around fancily decorated stalls playing games, trying to win items on display, throwing flannel balls, lighting candles with one match to win prizes such as bottles of Trinidad rum, perfumes, teddy bears. He was always trying to impress me. He didn't have to. We couldn't wait to go to the disco dance later that evening. From about 7pm, we picked a corner inside the crowded hall, and danced all night for three hours. Our friends occasionally checked in on us, then later said goodbye. After school, we were often seen together frequenting ice cream shops, and Mario's Pizzeria. In private, he mixed me Brandy Alexanders. He was the first to show me a world I had only read about or seen on T.V. For his age he was mature, a man. He made me know he wanted to have me beside him.

Just months later, when I was crowned Miss Providence 1979, Dexter was extremely proud, and even more so on some afternoons to drive up to school and pick me up. Dexter and I danced to each song on the Bee Gee's "Too Much Heaven" album which was given as first prize. He also took the gold Cross ballpoint pen set inscribed in curly letters *Miss Providence 1979*, and kept it with him. He was happier when we walked together, and boys from Dominic's Savio whispered "Miss Providence" close to my ear. He quickly warded them off, letting them know I belonged to him. Winning my first beauty crown after competing with several rivals was precious. I learnt while women were often seen as physical objects first, we had to work hard to prove we were much more than our looks. I knew under the façade of beauty, I would always be more. With his uncle, friends, and sometimes family members we spent weekends in the country, planning trips to Manzanilla beach, Mayaro, and Toco.

Dexter possessed a contagious eagerness for living. He knew how to treat people well, and then I understood why he was so popular. After high school graduation, and getting accepted into Corpus Christi College of Occupational Education and Training, Dexter was still at my side, driving me to school, making great plans for our future together. He often spoke about our future lives – how it would be... openly fantasising about the house in Maracas he would build for us. He was ambitious and wanted the best of everything for me. By that time I had already met his mother, knew she was well travelled, and shopped abroad for a boutique "Jan's" she owned and operated under Salvatori Building in Port-of-Spain. His mother Janet was lovely and energetic, easy to like. Dexter promised me he would get me a job working with his mother. He loved her, and lived for her to approve of him seeing me. I think she did. If she did not, I didn't feel it in her presence. Even though we attended family gatherings together, I kept myself in the background, talking with his young sister Nicole or either of his two brothers, Brian and Michael. He was the first of four. His cousin Junior was his confidant, always steps away. Family gatherings were a huge affair; lovely Indian women were all exquisitely dressed, gathered around long lavish tables filled with spicy Indian dishes and delicacies. Their faces were perfectly made up, and they took centre stage. Beforehand, I had to let Dexter know what I intended to wear. Sometimes he bought me a new outfit to wear; I modelled the outfit for him as he looked on intently, and then awaited his approval.

But one Friday morning in late November, I was destined to wake up from a beautiful dream that never was to become reality. It was about 6am when I heard a familiar car horn blowing outside; Dexter's. Confused with sleep still in my eyes, I approached him. I remember he had this look of happiness and contentment. He told me he simply came to take me to school because he had to work, and would be late that evening in seeing me. He patiently waited in the car while I excitedly dressed. Once in the car, he reached over and kissed me. It was a soft lingering kiss. We didn't say much; he held my hand for most of the ride to school. When we got up to school, Dexter insisted I give him a good long kiss. I was panicked and didn't want to oblige. If any of the nuns saw us or worse if any student reported seeing us in a compromising situation, just before school started, I would have been in big trouble. My boyfriend was adamant. He pulled me over to his side, hugged me and gave me a deep long kiss. I was flushed because I didn't understand the reason for his early morning affection. I spent the entire day at school smiling for no reason.

During the day my thoughts were constantly on Dexter. He made me really happy that morning; I couldn't wait until the evening to see him. But he never came. I grew worried, fell asleep sometime later after 10pm. Just about midnight the same night, after falling asleep because he had not come by, I heard a loud deep voice, "Goodnight, goodnight." Following the last echo, I scrambled out of bed, and immediately became nervous the moment I saw a tall dark gentleman standing outside near our Guava tree. The figure didn't move. On approaching him, I recognised the man, having seen him before at one of Dexter's family gatherings. From the way he looked my gut told me something bad was about to unfold. My stomach became filled with butterflies. Speaking slowly without looking directly at me, the man confirmed my suspicions when he said there was an accident earlier that day on the North Coast where they had been working. The yellow backhoe Dexter had been driving turned over; he was pinned below. That evening Dexter died at the hospital. The man who brought the bad news to me walked away leaving me alone screaming hysterically, waking the household.

Dexter was buried on Monday December 3, 1980. Dressed in white Indian cotton dress flowing past my ankles, which his mother gave me to wear, I walked up the stairs and approached the shiny casket in which he lay. I wasn't afraid, because I had visited him in the morgue, and together with his mother, helped pick out his clothing, and got him dressed. It was only the second time I had been so close to a dead person, someone who I cared for deeply. He was cold and numb; so was I for many years after his death. Standing beside him, seeing him lying still inside a casket, I bent over and kissed his cheeks, then I sprayed him with the scent he so loved, Paco Rabanne. The smell remained with me. There were hundreds at his funeral, especially young people, some of whom were dressed in school uniforms. That dreadful day I didn't recognise anyone. What I remembered was Charlotte's lovely voice singing "Bridge over Troubled Waters".

Days after his burial, when Dexter returned to me in spirit calling my name, it was to his sweet scent I answered. He was everywhere I went. For weeks his fragrance followed me; I spoke loudly to him in my sleep. My grandmother knew what was happening because I slept next to her. One night, months later, I must have been having a dream in which I crept out of the bed, and started to follow my love, telling him I was coming. At that moment my grandmother intervened, cursing the dead, waking me, and telling Dexter to go and rest. She told him that I had a life without him, and he could not take me away because it was not my time. Then my grandmother called on Jesus and Mary, Mother of God, asking them to take care of the situation. I didn't remember anything the next morning, except what my family related to me. My Uncle Daniel, who didn't believe in the power of the spirit world, joked around saying "Dexter came to take you away last night, and Tina put a stop to it!"

In the time that followed, I was no good to anyone, not even myself. No amount of consolation from friends and family could make up for what was left empty inside of me. The pain was unimaginable, words a waste. I lived like a zombie doing things without meaning, living my life as if nothing mattered anymore. I learnt to cope with the pain of my love's death mostly on my own, by being alone, by living each day as it dawned without wanting anything, without giving anything, and without hoping there might be anything else left for me in this life.

Chapter 12

Facing the World of Work

"Sometimes you wake up. Sometimes the fall kills you. And sometimes when you fall you fly."

Neil Gaiman

It was early December 1980 when I started work at Hilton Hotel, a Tuesday, one day after my love's funeral. I was bleeding profusely; I bled for two more weeks. This was how my physical body reacted to trauma. But I had to attend to job training; it was the third job in our programme. The idea was to prepare us for the world of work beginning first at the bottom, working our way up the corporate ladder to banks and offices. My first job placement was at Hi Lo Supermarket. At the grocery we learnt how to clean and pack grocery shelves, label and upkeep goods, remove spoilt items or opened packages, package fresh items, cash, and supervise departments. This was a particularly positive experience because while we gained hands on experience, it fostered good working relationships with adults. I didn't have a bad experience on job training except one or two guys saying they liked me, and wanted to take me out. But while on the job, we were not allowed to date.

Working on cash was another learning experience because at the end of the day, the cashier was responsible for any shortage discovered on cash. So this method forced us to be vigilant; some of us learnt painstakingly that it might be better to finish up at the end of a day's take with more cash, than less than the register's tally. If the cash didn't match the register's printed receipt, a report had to be written up, then there were meetings with the supervisor, manager and the individual received strict warnings about being careful when at the cash register.

As young girls we had the chance to dress up as working adults wearing uniforms, make-up, and fancy shoes with matching handbags. For grocery work we wore gabardine pants suits in burgundy and navy. What I enjoyed most was applying make-up; eventually we became our own pros matching shades of blue, and green eye colour with wine colored lipsticks, and hues of pink. Some girls were just horrible at applying their own make-up; once at work they relied on me.

From the supermarket experience, we were sent in groups for training at factories. Among the factories included were: John Dickenson (stationery); Hands Arnold (appliances); Elite (clothing) and others. I reported for job training at Mayfair Knitting Industries (stockings and socks) located in the Diamond Vale Industrial Estate, only about twenty minutes from where I lived in Petit Valley. Crystal Stream divided Morne Coco Road and Diego Martin Main Road. Every morning I walked across Crystal Stream, and stood at the corner of Diego Martin Main Road near Rain-O-Rama (Lord Kitchener's home), where I waited for a taxi to take me to Diego Martin.

At Mayfair Knitting, and while we sometimes worked gruelling graveyard shifts from 10pm to 7am, we had enough time after work to rest and recover for the next day. At the factory we tended to spinning machines being careful not to get our hands caught between heavy machinery, stretched the stay-ups, looking out for snags in the nylon, packaged, and counted boxes. As young women the experience also gave us another close-up glimpse into the world of work, helping us to mature even faster. We learnt to appreciate things; whenever we saw a pair of stockings or socks we had a vivid image of how it became hosiery in the first place. I remember our bosses at Mayfair were not as welcoming or nice as those we left at Hi Lo supermarket; the factory environment was much more restrictive. There were no random breaks, lunch was only thirty minutes, and we quickly discovered the pay was significantly lower. We had to undergo our own period of adjustment, to learn what we needed to as part of the commitment to occupational education. It was my first peek into factory life, its difficulties, low wages, harsh working conditions, and lack of employee benefit plans. At the end of each job session all earnings from the entire work programme were collected and equally divided among participating students.

Writing job reports at the end of every training session was not easy or even pleasant. Writing those reports was important to the job training programme. For one thing the Job Training Officer could also make her own assessment from the report, as well as she could use the opportunity to speak with bosses to ensure there were no reccurrences of bad or less pleasant incidents. I remember having to relate an incident; I witnessed a manager being extremely insensitive to a pregnant woman because she often fell ill. Early in the day and since the factory became hot and stuffy because overhead fans were limited, the woman explained she felt like fainting. But when she headed towards the bathroom, explaining to the manager how nauseated she felt, he stood in front of her, blocking her path, and cautioned her if she took another break, she had to remove her handbag and things from the premises, and not return. I would not forget the expression on the employee's face as she helplessly returned to her workstation. Only days later, as a result of another incident regarding a bathroom break she needed, the employee was fired. Then there were other incidents where one of the supervisors made sexual passes at a few of us, inviting us to go out with him. One girl was even taken out of the factory training because she gave in to the temptation. After reports to the job training officer were filed against her, she admitted to going out after work with the supervisor. She was severely reprimanded, and for a period of time not allowed to return to job training.

These experiences made me in my teenage years notice how harshly some women were treated at work; in fact they were not respected for their contribution, especially if they became pregnant; I realised early there was not always fair play on the job, how hard women had to work to gain respect, and especially the fact that some men in positions of power dominated over women on the job scene. Some employers took advantage of women's vulnerabilities. From my early teenage job experience, I became appalled with the treatment many women endured and believed in some way I could make things better. After all, I also saw first hand how everything on the job mostly depended on women, and especially how women always did their part and more. This was not what I heard; I lived it first hand on the job. In my youth I was beginning to understand many facts about the world of work, about women, and especially about men.

At Hilton Hotel the experience was worth every penny we were paid at the end of our training. There we learnt about hotel operations, shifts, and once again worked in different areas. Starting with housekeeping, which was not usually a pleasant task, we had to first learn the job. Clients often left soiled sheets, underwear, and condoms for us to pick up after them. While some guests were neat and tidy, the majority were dirty, and often downright shameful. I suppose they figured they were paying for service at the hotel. But it was a job with which we had to become familiar. From housekeeping, we moved to the kitchen, which was extremely busy and demanding. Apart from working side by side with wonderful chefs and cooks, we took customer orders, served meals and cleared tables at the Pool Terrace, and also the famous Restaurant "La Boucan." There we intermingled with foreigners, and native Trinidadians who dropped by for lunchtime meals, mid-afternoon tea or dinner. Hilton was the place where even locals celebrated birthdays, anniversaries, or breakups, where some husbands who cheated on their wives brought their mistresses, and sometimes we observed wives did the same. Once someone left one nickel on the table, and I wondered what prompted them to be so mean to waiters and waitresses? It was better they hadn't left anything; one nickel was an insult to all of us.

Chefs were always busy planning, baking, and peeling. Kitchen talk was good. They welcomed our help and prepared every dish; we of course had the fine chance of tasting. It was at Hilton I ate so much fresh pineapple my gums remained sore for days. Workers kept us busy and in good moods by joking around, playing music, and dancing while they worked; you actually developed a liking for the kitchen, while at the same time appreciating the hard work done there long after cooking and serving was over. At cleanup time, local calypso music kept us busy washing large dishes, scrubbing counters, and mopping floors.

Holidays and parties were another way we prepared more fancy dishes and acquired foreign tastes. It was at Hilton I tasted Brussel Sprouts for the first time. We were serving at a Christmas banquet dinner, a spacious dining hall, elaborately decorated, in the middle of which stood a snowman made of ice; he was more than ten feet in the air. My friends dared me to taste the Brussels Sprouts. The tiny cabbage-like vegetable was nicely piled into a fancy bowl. Taking the dare, I slid under the table hidden by flowing lace tablecloth, and quickly put one into my mouth; first I sucked then bit into the warm moist vegetable. The instant I got the bitter taste, I spat it out under the table, making a loud "Yuck!" sound. Everyone laughed at me. Deep in my heart while I appeared to be having fun, the taste in my mouth reminded me of my bittersweet experience losing Dexter. It was only weeks since his burial, and everything I did, was done with thoughts of him watching me from far away. I was quietly living in pain, learning well how to mask it, to go on with life as if there was not a large hole in my heart, because from where I stood everyone seemed to be moving along with their own lives. I discovered how strong my survival instincts actually were because I was determined to heal.

At the bar, we learnt to mix cocktails and drinks, some general bar etiquette about customers, observing when it became necessary to warn guests about drinking and having to drive, or having to walk them to their rooms after spending hours drinking and listening to their life stories. The men who trained us at the bar were extremely professional, worked at the hotel for many years, and related some of their experiences dealing with customers. At reservations we had to be a little more professional in our manner of approach, since we were constantly being observed by customers as well as managers. I soon decided on our next job training I would not work at banks when the time came around, because I didn't like pretending I was having a good day when I wasn't, and I also didn't like passing on my anger to people who didn't deserve it. While I was still fragile, the job experience helped put things about life into perspective; I matured faster. Moreover, the kind-hearted staff we encountered while being trained left a lasting impression in our minds. I don't remember whether the staff at Hilton knew about my recent loss, but they taught me how to move on with life, in particular *there was hope; all was not lost; life went on, and most of all, people are generally nice, and want to be good.* While job training at Hilton Hotel I met some of the nicest people I have in my life.

I started reflecting on my job experience, and wondered about how lucky I was, and especially how proud of me Dexter would have been. Months before entering the world of work, we had been trained by army personnel who came to our school for fitness instructions followed by our training at Tetron Army Base. Twice weekly two army trucks drove up to our school; we boarded and were driven down to the army base in Chaguaramas. Imagine the sight of young schoolgirls all dressed in army green khaki overalls, sitting just like soldiers at the back of trucks. At Tetron we were placed in groups according to what aspects of auto mechanics interested us. Some students opted for welding, others chose electrical installations, and I joined the straightening and spray-painting group. For months we learnt, observed, were tested and produced a product; each group worked on damaged vehicles brought into the shop for repairs. Working alongside army personnel was stimulating. It gave us a chance as young women to question things, to see whether we could also perform similar duties as the kind relegated to mostly men; to push our limits and learning capabilities; to create a sense of positivity and accomplishment while working in a highly disciplined environment. We made our trainers proud.

In the final job placement before graduation from Corpus Christi College I worked at a private office, Beta Enterprises Limited, an Air-conditioning, Refrigerating, Sales and Service Company. For about three years after graduation, I remained in the position as Secretary to the Service Department Manager. At the office I learnt many more things about the world of work, and especially about myself. There were only two women working among fifteen men. This was not difficult. By that time, I was almost twenty, and had grown accustomed to working among men, and being challenged by them. This was another learning experience. We were nurtured and protected. We were efficient, and I discovered I was an independent self-sufficient worker. Whether or not my two bosses were present I performed all duties assigned to me; I could be relied upon to make decisions, give advice and follow up situations with customers. I realised when left alone I worked best, and further, whatever I did with my life would always depend on my choices. I trusted myself to survive.

It was during the period of working at Beta, when I first met Anthony. He was a young man I had been eying every morning as he drove past me at Crystal Stream. From a distance I could see the white RX2 approaching. I think every young man in the early eighties who could drive, and had the choice of owning a car, chose an RX2 because they could make it really fancy with huge mag wheels and rims, souped up engine, and striking paint. If they had money, they instead opted for an RX7. Anthony passed at the same time every morning, and on this particular morning, quite unexpectedly; he just stopped at the corner of Diego Martin Main Road and Crystal Stream Avenue, and offered me a ride into Port-of-Spain. We had not formally met, only flirted with each other as he drove past me every day. But that morning I stepped into his car because there was someone else in the car. It was funny how he introduced me to his father, who was sitting in the front seat. Since we hadn't formally met he said, "Dad this is…" with a long pause waiting for me to reply "Sue-Ann." I introduced myself from the back seat, and he looked up at me from his mirror and smiled. For the entire ride as we crawled in traffic, Anthony kept staring at me from the mirror; sometimes our eyes met, and I also smiled.

I gave him directions about where to drop me off. He did and so we didn't have the chance to talk. Around lunch time that same day at work Anthony pulled up in front of my office, requesting my phone number, and also offering to pick me up in the afternoon. I agreed. When she met him, my girlfriend Ann-Marie told me to give him a chance; he seemed nice. Most of all, he was driving a car; he could pick me up and take me places. That morning ride in Anthony's white Mazda turned into a romantic relationship that lasted four years. While our romance was real, it was much different than the previous one I had shared with Dexter.

Chapter 13

"Yes I do."

"No matter what happens, keep on beginning and failing. Each time you fail, start all over again, and you'll grow stronger until you find you have accomplished a purpose – Not the one you began with perhaps, but one you will be glad to remember."

Anne Sullivan

Anthony and I got engaged on September 28th 1985 after dating for three years. Our wedding was planned for one year later on September 28th, 1986. I believed I was ready to give myself to someone for the rest of my life, Anthony. We knew mostly everything about each other, finished each other's sentences, spent time together visiting my mother in Tobago for long weekends and holidays. Isn't that what girls dream of and boys live for? My family liked Anthony; he was likeable. We both had good jobs. Eventually I left Beta Enterprises because my Aunt Rose got me a better paying job at Colibri Jewelry. The Head Office was located in Diamond Vale Industrial Estate, the same area where I had worked on job training at Mayfair Knitting. The first time her boss interviewed me, I was hired on the spot, and reported for work within the next few days. My Aunt Rose told her boss he would not be disappointed in me. Her boss offered me a better salary package including benefits such as health insurance, paid vacation, and once we passed the probationary period of three months, and became permanently employed we each received an annual travel allowance of $1800. The boss encouraged his staff to use the money for world travel. He wanted us to see what an interesting place the world was. From the beginning I was impressed by this offer of employment. The owners were a group of three male partners: one who managed factory operations; one who was responsible for stock, buying and selling gold, silver, precious and semi-precious stones, and the Personnel boss who dealt with hiring, firing, retailing and store operations. From time to time their tasks overlapped. The three got along very well together and when I joined the company, they owned about three stores located in Malls across Trinidad. By the time I worked for two years, the owners made millions, adding three more stores to their name. They were good men who compensated their employees fairly.

I was stationed at the Head Office, and enjoyed my job as a Junior Accounts Clerk. The working environment was familiar, having previously worked in Accounts. My job description included handling payroll for factory workers after tallying their time cards each week. Their wages were small and so it was difficult to make deductions out of already meagre wages. The process got to me so much that in some instances, I just didn't make the deductions I was supposed to. When I explained this to my supervisor, she told me not to worry about it, but I had to at least make some deductions. So I did. By the time workers received their reduced paychecks on Friday, they returned to the office on Monday for loans, which through the office's petty cash were made available to them. Perhaps it was my job training at school that made me empathetic to workers' circumstances on the job, or maybe it was just my inner sense of fairness and integrity. In trying to do the best job I did not want to betray my boss's trust.

Anthony worked in Port-of-Spain so we didn't see each other during the day. On special holidays some of us who worked at the factory were assigned to jewellery stores in the Malls. I longed for the change of scenery, and the idea of having to deal one-on-one with customers. We were adequately compensated for working extra hours. Once at the shop, we had to work different shifts according to the Mall hours, usually until 9pm. On such occasions Anthony picked me up after work. Our boss had a knack for hiring beautiful young women of all ethnic and social backgrounds. Their shops were sprinkled with friendly lovely looking young women, many of whom were single. We decorated our bodies with pieces of jewellery we sold, and were also allowed to purchase items at factory price, each of us having a credit account. At the jewellery store, I learnt about precious metals and gem stones. Sapphire reminded me of the deep blue sky; ruby of Indian garments; diamond was my mother's birth stone; opal and citrine were calming.

It was my travel allowance together with monetary gifts that allowed Anthony and me a wonderful honeymoon in Puerto Rico, USA where we spent eight glorious nights at the Regency in San Juan. It was a surprise gift for a delighted fiancé. We had no problem obtaining USA visas. At that time we had no plans whatsoever of remaining outside our homeland, let alone settling anywhere in the world. Everything we needed and loved was in Trinidad. We had our entire lives before us. Once they saw us together, it was easier to convince the USA Immigration officers we had no intention of remaining in the USA.

My boss was a good man; he wanted his staff to be happy. He said he believed thinking that way will get him more value for his money. Whenever we were ill he said it didn't matter how long you stayed away from the job, when a person was ill, he/she was ill. In many ways I admired him for his outlook; it seemed unusual. He was well travelled, married a French woman, and was influenced by the outside world; he created a culture of his own for good.

Anthony and I were seriously dating. It was 1982. He wasn't the kind of person who visited you once, took you out, and then forgot about you. He was constantly dropping by to take you somewhere, a cricket match, car racing, and beach barbecues. He once rode a 250 four-stroke Yamaha, but by the time we met, he had sold it, and decided he wouldn't ride for a while until he made enough money to buy himself a 1,000 Kawasaki. He related some motor cycle incidents to me, one in which there was an accident, and his previous girlfriend was flung from the back of the motorcycle unto the bonnet of an oncoming vehicle. Another incident happened when he was travelling late at night, and fell asleep, riding close between two vehicles, almost getting crushed in the process, waking up in enough time to manoeuvre himself to safety. He wasn't sure how he survived those experiences, and I suppose for a while he decided to play it safe with life.

We saw each other every night. He visited me at my grandmother's place in Crystal Stream. I realized the white RX2, he drove was bought with his own earnings. Like most young men, he also lived for his hard earned car. Whenever he came to visit me, we mostly watched T.V. He talked with my uncles, and we waited for some of the household to go to sleep, so we could make out. Anthony was not the outspoken type; he was reserved, mostly quiet. But once you started a conversation with him, it would be a good talk. He knew a lot about cars, auto mechanics, and office machinery. He had some special gift for fixing cars. Someone was always calling on him, whenever their vehicle stalled somewhere on the road; he often left to help someone, or he didn't show up to pick me up because he was fixing someone's vehicle. He eventually showed up exhausted and disheveled with dirty hands. Sometimes because I chose not to believe his stories our conversation ended in big fights with us ending up vexed with each other for some extended period of time until someone, anyone, apologised first. Then after a few days we started our relationship all over again, acting as if nothing happened, professing our deep love for each other. Whenever my grandmother didn't see him come by for a few days, she asked me about what I did to make him angry; my grandmother never believed he did something to make me angry.

Over the course of the four years we dated, we travelled to Tobago several times to visit my mother, stepfather, and brother. One weekend we took the *Panorama* to Tobago, a boat that made the trip in about six hours. We took a cabin, but slept the entire trip. When we awoke it was near 8am everything was still. Embarrassed we quickly gathered our stuff, and tried to make a quiet exit. To our surprise, all the passengers had left since 5am a.m. As we bolted off the boat there were cleaners, and deck hands mopping the boat. It appeared to us they were having a good laugh at our expense, you know two young lovers alone in a cabin; who would have believed we slept the entire trip!

Once during summer vacation we went to Tobago. We took Anthony's car packed it with groceries, rented a house belonging to one of my mother's friends, and had a blast of a time. At midnight we got ready to go crab hunting. It was a fun-filled adventure; we carried torches and rope. We chased huge blue crabs away from their holes, caught them, were run down by them with their loop like eyes slanted, and huge *Gundies* open and ready, threw them into the car trunk, or cracked their backs and dropped the leaking remnants of crab into a plastic bucket. There was no surprise my brother loved to chase me around holding the crab in his hand laughing, while I screamed uncontrollably. The next day, we would have to be careful walking around the house just in case a crab or two got out of the trunk. It might get hold of a toe or something – that would be crazy because when that crab's Gundy grabs hold of something it didn't let go. It was interesting watching how excited my brother became breaking crab backs, saying "another broken back," giggling, throwing it into the bucket. We scrubbed and cleaned the crabs, washed them with green lime, and seasoned them with mixed herbs. Crabs made mouth-watering curry crab and dumplings, or are preferred adding a delightful flavour to *callalloo*, the local soup blend.

My mother and stepfather got along well with Anthony; from early my mother hinted to me she believed he was the one for me. When I asked her how she knew that, she said by experience. He had become my safety net; he was caring, and was there for me. At the time, I didn't love him the way I loved Dexter; I trusted I eventually would. He had met me just after breaking up with his girlfriend, and I met him not long after Dexter's death. We both needed to be needed, and in that way we became good for each other. By the time I met his family and two older sisters we were seeing each other for more than two years, spending holidays, birthdays, sharing in his parents anniversaries, and other family gatherings.

Anthony came from a medium sized family, mainly with Chinese and Creole background. His mother was Woon Sam, his father Commissiong, carrying the name made famous by 1977 Miss Universe, Trinidad's Janelle Penny Commissiong. His family name spread across Portugal, France, Italy, Grenada, and some other Caribbean islands. One of his uncles, his Aunt Sandra's husband, who was also his godfather was a successful businessman. As is the custom, he eventually built a home in China in thanksgiving for all he had accomplished. Sadly, only a few years ago, this uncle was tragically gunned down in his own driveway in Trinidad. I met his uncle Christopher several times in our years together. He was a good man; he loved his family; he was generous, and had his own way.

In some ways his uncle reminded me of my Uncle Daniel, tending to family needs and being financially responsible. But much unlike my uncle, their family owned several business enterprises and were well off. As an outsider looking in, his Uncle Christopher was a traditional kind of man, whose ways could not be easily changed; you had to accept him for who he was – you had to adjust to him; he would not bend his ways to accept you. That was all. Around him, I never felt like an outsider. In the brief moments we shared at family gatherings, he was warm, told family stories, and was also a good cook. Uncle Christopher also blessed my union with Anthony. He believed in me, and some of the things I freely shared with him; I loved this man. It's funny how the people who make the most impact on our lives, those whose perfume leave lasting scents either move miles away from us or die.

Anthony and I were engaged in 1985. We had a mass at St. Anthony's and dinner at his family's home in Diamond Vale. Immediately after our engagement, I began planning for our wedding scheduled for one year later, September 1986. I started randomly jotting things down as they came to mind. Before long I had pages of notes, things to check out, and people to call. I started asking questions and before long had a pretty good start on planning our own wedding. I realised in our own family, there was support. Auntie Yvonne could help with the cakes, some of my aunts could gather and decide on the menu, our friend Betty whose husband, Curtis was a photographer could take photographs, Anthony's family would cater the bar, and mine would handle food and all other arrangements. It was the way most Christian weddings were organised in Trinidad.

I first made enquiries then solid bookings: dates and times for the hall, church, choir and travel, way in advance, making careful notes of required down payments. I ordered flowers, and shopped around for someone to decorate and ice the wedding cake, which my mother, Aunt Angela together with Aunt Yvonne would bake. Aunt Yvonne was my mother's first cousin on granny's side. Like Aunt Angela, she was also extremely talented and creative. She made me many clothes: dresses, jackets and skirts from fabric I brought her. She sewed wedding outfits, drapery and sheets. She and I got along very well, and while I waited for her she offered me delicious homemade coconut ice cream and sponge cake.

My sister and I flew to Venezuela to shop for silks, shoes, hosiery, lace, gloves, jewellery, gifts and trinkets. When my grandmother heard the news about our upcoming marriage, she was overjoyed. That day, she opened a drawer inside her closet and gave me in my hand some $2,200 in cash. I was shocked. My grandmother's words were "This is for your dress; I was saving it for you." The money was crisp and hidden inside neatly folded articles of clothing. It was clear that she must have been saving for years, since not only was I one of her favourite grand's, but I had not left my grandmother's side. Family chipped in and gave us money for shopping in Venezuela. We had a family member, Vijay Singh who married a Venezuelan woman, Oneida; when we got to Venezuela, we were welcome at their home, which was a long bus ride from Caracas. My sister and I had a wonderful time together, roaming wide streets in Caracas, shops, admiring how well dressed Spanish women were. Although my sister hated shopping she knew this was important, so she kept her promise of being there for me.

When we returned home from Venezuela, there was work to be done. My Aunt Angela had the most important task. Her job was to create and design my wedding dress with yards and yards of lovely fabric, lace trimmings, beads and things we purchased. In the next few months I spent nights with my Aunt Angela, watching her out of pure love, cut from paper a pattern, cut fabric by hand, and sew my wedding dress, fitting my skinny body to perfection. We made my veil; it was a lace and beaded white cap that fitted in the centre of my head, and flowed into white netting to the length of the dress. The dress was hand-beaded; I was honored to wear my aunt's own creation.

Anthony and I were getting married months later in September. Since it was only months after my stepfather's death, I asked my mother whether we should postpone the wedding, but because we had already sent out invitations, she insisted we should continue with our wedding plans intimating to us life had to go on.

I knew my mother could not be there for us in the way we had anticipated, but I understood her pain. My stepfather was also not present in the physical state. I realised something though about death and dying. I didn't know what the answer was, but I was sure there was some deep communication between the person who was about to die, and the people they're closest to.

Having suffered and lived through the experience of my boyfriend, Dexter's death in November 1980, I was somehow made ready to cradle my mother when my stepfather, whom she loved, and lived with since leaving us, passed away. That happened in July 1986. In the beginning, the lessons I internalized through these events bent me shapeless, but over time, these unfortunate events helped me to understand and interpret life. I handled, with my sister's help, all the funeral arrangements for my mother, which included making lists, getting money together to pay the funeral parlour for renting space, purchasing the casket and accessories, and taking care of my stepfather's body. I purchased things like handkerchiefs, flowers, incense and candles, organised seven nights of prayer, took care of the undertakers, cemetery and church arrangements including creating a programme for the service, and grocery shopped. I remember picking out my stepfather's last set of clothing, his favourite cotton shirt, a tweed blazer from England, and matching pants. I wanted him to look especially sharp for what was to be the last time my mother, friends and family would see him. Hardest of all, I had to watch my mother; to ensure that though she was distraught, she was taken care of. What I realised was because of my past experience with Dexter's death, I was no longer afraid of the dead, speaking with the undertaker, making final burial arrangements. Without medication, my mother was in a trance, and remained in that state even after my wedding day in late September of that same year. Letting go, I knew, would be very, very hard for her.

My stepfather and I had developed a close relationship. In fact for years I went so far as to ask my mother whether there was any chance he was my father, and she had hidden it from me. They both denied it, explaining when my mother left with my stepfather she did so leaving her three children behind. So I accepted I wasn't his daughter. I understood I loved him so dearly that I wanted to belong somewhere. While lying on his hospital bed the afternoon I passed my driving test and while he congratulated me, I asked my stepfather to walk me up the aisle for our wedding. But he didn't give me a definite answer. He did not say "Yes" as I wanted. I was put off by his non-committal response. In fact months before his surgery, he suggested I ask Uncle Harry, my grandmother's brother. My stepfather explained in detail Uncle Harry would be happy to do so since we were not strangers. I was hurt by my stepfather's refusal to walk me up the aisle on my wedding day. Only months later when he died did I realise he said this because deep down, perhaps in his unknowing, he recognised he might not have been there to share the occasion with us. Without hurting us more deeply, this was his way of communicating – his gesture of love. This is only my account of what I believed happened, and why I believe in the connection between those who are about to die and their loved ones. In the same way Dexter spent his last morning on earth driving me to school, kissing me, and taking time to remind me of his love for me; in fact he also visited his mother and some of his relatives that morning. Unknown to us, they communicated with those they love.

Two weekends before the wedding, Anthony's friends treated him to his bachelor party down at Chaguaramas where we heard they were just crazy young men and friends drinking, partying and playing weird pranks on the groom-to-be. This event was held at the ocean front so they had no difficulty throwing each other into the water! The shower was held for me at my Uncle Harry's place; it was a surprise. The girls gave me a really hard time since I was extremely private and usually took offence to obscene jokes. It was a laughing and crying kind of night, all at the same time. Many of my girl friends made themselves little fools for one night of pure fun and playfulness.

edding day, September 28th, 1986, I arrived at the
ιe Nativity on the stroke of 4pm not a minute later. I
.. For three months before, I attended several sessions at
.te of Beauty. This was a spa run by Rachel Ann Thomas,
ιauty queen who represented Trinidad and Tobago in Miss
Woɪ៶. I had facials and steams. One of their make-up artists named Cheryl came to our home to apply my make-up. She worked at the Institute and we became friends. Curtis took photographs the moment I emerged in bathrobe from the shower until I was dressed in full splendour. Roy, a hairstylist who worked with many fashion models, styled my hair earlier that morning. We shared breakfast with Anthony's family at our home. More than 300 hundred family and guests applauded my early arrival, including my school Principal Sr. Petronilla Joseph. She said I made her extremely proud; it was the mark of a Corpus Christi graduate. Singing in the church choir for years, seeing anxious husbands waiting on their brides sometimes for more than an hour, I always told myself I would never be late for my wedding. *Why would I want to keep the man I intended on spending the rest of my life with waiting, and sweating at the altar, wondering whether or not I changed my mind.* Our two favourite parish priests, Fr. Knolly Knox, and Fr. Tom Lawson performed the ceremony, the choir sang, we lighted two candles together joining separate flames into one single flame, symbolising our oneness. Standing before hundreds of witnesses, we vowed our eternal love for each other. My sister was chief bridesmaid, together with my best friend, Joanne Hernandez. My sister was radiant in her gold silk skirt and Chinese collar patterned blouse. She was perfectly made up and her hair was nicely done. Imagine my sister all decked up in fashion, stockings and high heels. There were three bridesmaids, one flower girl, Angie's last, my god daughter Kerry-Ann accompanied by four handsomely dressed escorts, and one pageboy, my cousin Christian. As planned, special moments of our wedding were videotaped.

The celebrations following the church ceremony, and dinner

was held at Lion's Civic Center in Port-of-Spain. A lavish dinner was prepared with Indian food on one side of the buffet, and Chinese food on the other. The hall was beautifully decorated in varying hues of yellow, white and gold. Wedding favours were handmade from plastic bottles with nicely arranged matching bouquets of flowers inserted inside the bottles. Everyone was present, employees and bosses from Anthony's job; friends from my job; church people, close family friends, and family on both sides. Anthony and I walked around to each table thanking people for attending and sharing the occasion with us. We were separated for a while during the evening, drinking champagne and toasting with our friends.

After the formalities of speeches, cutting the wedding cake, throwing the bouquet, and dancing to our wedding song "Here and Now", by Luther Vandross, and when the party was in full swing, I changed into a handmade skirt in cobalt and white silk. The top was low-cut with most of my back exposed, the skirt was long and closely fitting. We danced and danced late into the night. The hall was booked until twelve; the party went on after midnight. We got a ride to Bel Air, the hotel near the airport, where we spent the night. Intimately, whatever was supposed to happen on one's wedding night never did. Both Anthony and I were too happily exhausted to do anything, but hold each other closely and sleep. We had an early wake up call to catch a flight for San Juan, Puerto Rico. Puerto Rico was the place where we intended to share our wedded bliss.

Chapter 14

Raffick

A child growing up away from the warmth, love and stability of family is a different child. I grew up separated at a young age from my family. Since then I've always seen things differently. When you're alone you learn early that you must survive; there's a debt you want to repay yourself. As far as I can remember, I've been a loner. I walked away from big family gatherings, friends or anyone wanting to get too attached to me. I found churches, riverbanks and gardens where I retreated. I convinced myself I was strong. I didn't need anyone to complete my life. I discovered early in life how much depended on me, the company I kept, and especially the choices I made. At eleven when I wrote the eleven plus examination and passed for a prestige school, I was convinced that on my own, I could really pull off this thing called *life*.

High school was an adventure. I was the model of perfection – bright, bony, and friendly. Teachers adored my serious attitude; in many ways they capitalised on it. I became Miss Providence 1977, and for two years after Providence Girls High School was head girl at Corpus Christi College. I was an active member of the Legion of Mary, the school choir, drama club and debate team. I played hockey, lawn tennis and ran relay in sports. I had many friends, was one of the most popular girls, was liked and hated at the same time and met my first love at sixteen. But though those things were important, and helped me shape my world view, perhaps nothing prepared me for the realities I'd face in life, many of which, I realise, are still constantly changing. While much of who I was then made me who I am today, I remain awakened for the life before me.

Whenever my father visited with us at my grandmother's in Petit Valley, he brought me leather sandals from Brazil, trinkets from Surinam or Guyana, and many sea creatures in the form of ornaments like star fish, crabs and sea horses. His hugs lasted only brief moments. During his visits, he also brought my grandmother fresh fish and shrimp. Depending on what time of day he arrived, if she hadn't already cooked, my grandmother immediately started to cut, wash, and season the sea catch. On his visits with us, he left my grandmother some money, and while chatting with her, he sternly eyed me asking my grandmother whether I was good, did my schoolwork, and was listening to her. My grandmother always assured him I was the best.

On his return trips home, my father didn't talk much about what the experience was like being out there in the middle of the ocean where sea and sky seem to meet, where unexpected storms hit, nights were dark and lonely or men booze up for days and nights getting high enough to keep them from feeling lonely and missing families they left behind. He didn't talk about whether or not he missed his family, and in particular whether or not he missed me. I imagined working on a ship must have been difficult, frightening and challenging. These were the kinds of jobs men took or believed they had to do to prove they were strong men. Since my mother's leaving, I wasn't sure whether my father insisted he had to prove something or make something of himself by taking a job far off from the reality of his life. Maybe he wanted to.

Whenever he visited on free weekends my uncles, and friends they worked with at United Grocers, gathered with my father downstairs, playing games of all fours, mostly on Sundays. Each square table was set up with four chairs; they played in pairs. I strolled around tables, distributed points, brought glasses with ice, shared peanuts or depending on who was pairing up with who, just stood at my father's or my uncle Daniel's side for good luck. They said whenever I stood next to them they were dealt winning hands. If on the other hand they were losing, they jokingly chased me away.

I grew to accept this brief time with my father, never asking him about his whereabouts. Whenever he came by I was glad to see him, and when he left, well, he left. I decided early on my job was to live through the experience – to grow up. After a short stay, sometimes less than one week, my father left again for the ocean heading off to some distant land. He sailed on a boat called *The Bonanza*. That was all we knew. I never saw the vessel, or anyone with whom my father travelled, except for one man who we knew as Prince. But I wondered about those distant lands my father traveled to – how the sight of land must have excited the seamen just like in the movies – how lovely, scantily dressed, foreign women working at ports must have tempted the seamen, even my father. Deep inside I knew even if he hadn't already, one day my father would succumb to such temptations. When that day came I believed we wouldn't see him any longer, and there was nothing we could do.

After only a few years passed and my father visited with us less often than he did previously, I depended less and less on seeing him. Whenever I started having bad thoughts about him I quickly talked myself out of the dark pit, convincing myself it didn't matter, and I couldn't hate him because from what he told me, it was my mother who left home – he was my father. But I started to hide him far inside my mind, lived without him. Eventually he disappeared into a memory of something we once shared, far from perfect. Years passed, and we heard my father became friendly with a woman named Molly, who lived not far from us, only a fifteen minute walk from our home to Winnie

Mohammed Road. At least she was not a foreign woman I had found myself thinking. Whenever he returned from the sea, he no longer rushed to see us, but her. We visited him at her home where he stayed. Molly had children of her own whom we met. My sister first became close to her son, Ricardo who attended Petit Valley Boys' Catholic School. He rode a bicycle, and that was all Susan needed to lure herself into his life. After a few years, in 1973 when my father and mother divorced, he and Molly married. From their marriage my father and Molly had a daughter, Michelle. We had an extended family.

Visiting with my father at his new home was challenging. Though Molly was pleasant, her children friendly, my father could not see me as his growing daughter, and in fact he continued referring to me as his baby, the young one. Whenever the three of us visited, my father put us to sit in the gallery. He related stories about when my mother left him, how my mother was seeing someone else, and their break up was because of my mother. She walked out. She was unfaithful. He always said when we got older we would understand everything. He never realised we already did. What my father didn't know was my mother never discussed the circumstances of her leaving with any of us, let alone say cruel things about him. In fact my mother lived inside her own silence and guilt about what she did, hoping she could over years and through her actions make amends to us for her choices. These visits with our father became emotionally strained for us, especially if before our arrival my father had been drinking. Our stepmother came to sit with us in the gallery often commanding her husband to shut up, reminding him he had said enough. Our visits usually ended up with me crying, him saying "One day you'll be old enough to understand," and my brother and sister whisking me away.

Like both my siblings, I internalised those visits with my father because he insisted I was too young to understand anything. He didn't realise I was also growing up and figuring things out on my own. My brother Ricky was openly angry; he burst into fits of anger wanting a confrontation with our father, storming off through the gate, slamming the gate, and swearing he would never visit again. But he always showed up again and again. My brother was forgiving, and understood just like me, what he wanted most was our father's love. The way Susan internalised the visits with our father was to create her own internal world believing whatever she wanted to, and from time to time her feelings for both our parents wavered between love and hate and many confusing emotions that fell in between the two.

I, on the other hand, lived with my grandmother and her children who cradled me from about six until I graduated high school, became a young woman, and faced the working world. I had a strong Catholic upbringing, knew right from wrong, and was comfortable in my own skin. I was a positive person, always looking for some good outcome out of a not so good situation, believing hope was alive. Over the years, I developed a strong friendship with my mother and stepfather, and less frequently visited my father and his new family. From early and on my own without any psychological help, I decided not to harbour grudges inside of me for either parent. Sometimes years passed without me seeing my father and while I often wondered how he was doing or what was happening in his life, I didn't make much effort to visit him.

I remember my father had a particularly good handwriting. My sister Susan and I often sat at the kitchen table trying to write as he did; Susan tried without success to forge his signature; while she was becoming good at it, she was not near perfect. It was as if he attended some kind of special writing school and was the best. His letters were perfect script, legible with fancy capitals, curly endings, and a fascinating scrawl.

At twenty-three, after our engagement, I started planning our wedding and I knew the time had come to face my father again; I was now a young woman. I kept postponing visits, wanting it to go away. I knew deep inside I wanted him in my life, I wanted him to see his baby girl marry a handsome guy, and I wanted him to tell me how proud he was of me, and how much he loved me. *But how was I going to get that to happen? There were years separating us, where would I start?* I was scared to death to have to look him in the eye. By that time my uncles had nicknamed him "Black Dog" because he had in a way deserted us; they saw him more often than we did since they continued playing cards together or hung out at the savannah during horse racing events. Either my Uncle Daniel or Lincoln returned home and often mentioned "I saw Black Dog" today. On those occasions I was tempted to send messages with them to him about our wedding plans, but decided not to since it might anger him. I imagined the first thing he would say to them was "Tell her to come to me and relay the message herself."

Months passed until I finally decided it was time to visit with him and let him know about the wedding, while also introducing him to Anthony my fiancé. After explaining the scenario to Anthony, one afternoon he drove me to my father's place where together we sat in the gallery. Anthony and my father met. Immediately, my father started recounting the past, how we hadn't visited him in many years, how we went our own way, how my mother was responsible for all this, and before long I was engulfed with tears, wiping them away as fast as they flowed down soggy cheeks. Anthony was sitting closely hugging me. Once more my stepmother Molly came out to tell my father he had said enough. Anyway, I told him we were getting married, and I would invite him to the wedding because I wanted him there. Still in tears, and as we walked away, Anthony held my hand. I was relieved having gone to see him; it was over. No matter what happened next, I did my part. Now when the time came, all I had to do was drop off the wedding invitation. The rest was up to him.

My father had a big mouth, and it was no surprise news about our wedding immediately spread throughout his area. He told people his little girl was getting married. He didn't tell them he made me cry over and over, not letting go of the past, holding on to what was lost. He never mentioned what part he played in making us unhappy, making our visits to see him miserable, unbearable and filled with sadness. He didn't talk about what part he played in our mother's leaving, how unhappy their marriage had become, how badly he must have been treating her. My father was so blinded in self pity that he didn't notice his three children grew up before him. He didn't see they interpreted life on their own terms, and survived despite what was handed out to them by both parents.

My father eventually realised we could no longer be fooled; we had minds of our own, and as far as we could see our mother had done much more to make amends for her own choices. She didn't blame anyone but herself. She always told me whatever I wanted to do in life I could, but, I should always be prepared to face the consequences of my choices. I found out my father had put his hands on my mother on more than one occasion. She only told me this when I was engaged, about to be married. She was lecturing Anthony and me about how to treat each other, how to love each other rather than hurt each other. She warned Anthony never to put his hands on me.

My mother shared with us many details of her new life with my stepfather, after my father – how perfect their union was from the start. But whenever we visited them in Tobago she didn't have to convince us because the signs were there. My stepfather lived a full life with my mother, it was as if he did everything in this life for her, and there was nothing left to do, his purpose here was done. Even when he left this world for another unknown one he left deep markings on my own life – the way he filled a bucket of water and left it in the bathroom for my mother's bath; or put toothpaste on her toothbrush, and left it on the sink; his silent response to her rantings; his patient and wise responses to her confrontations. At night my stepfather filled two glasses with brandy, and after he showered waited inside for my mother. I would always know what time it was because he started to play love songs from their stereo. Three of his favourites were: "Cherish" by Kool and the Gang; "One in a Million" by Larry Graham; and Stevie Wonder's "I Just Called to Say I Love You". When I questioned my stepfather as to why Stevie Wonder's song was one of his favourites, he recalled some lyrics and with a heavenly grin my stepfather replied "The man is a genius!" He went on to explain the simplicity of the song and how deeply meaningful the lyrics were. That's what I loved about my stepfather, his depth was immense. We were two Earth signs: Taurus and Capricorn, bull and mountain goat. We got along pretty well. My mother told me she had never experienced such genuine and patient love from anyone, let alone my father with whom she bore three children. Amazing, how love changes its form every time.

Out of three hundred guests that included family and friends present at our wedding, I had no idea whether or not my father would show his face. He was not the one asked to walk me up the aisle, although thinking back I believe had I asked him he might have just to show off. My first choice was my stepfather; unfortunately he died in July only months before our wedding in September. My mother insisted we not postpone the wedding date. My stepfather's suggestion for my grandmother's older brother, Uncle Harry to walk me up the aisle came to pass; it all made sense. At the time he said Uncle Harry knew me from the time of my birth and watched me grow up; he was the perfect gentleman to walk me up the aisle. While I could not understand the reason my stepfather declined the offer, only months later I would realise he would not be present on our wedding day.

My Uncle Harry walked me up the aisle that day, me in my entire white splendour. He kissed me on the cheek and handed me over to Anthony who was waiting at the altar. I don't know whether my father witnessed that moment at the church, I secretly hoped he did. What it felt like seeing his little girl marrying I don't know either. But it was during the reception party when guests queued up to wish the bride and groom good luck, that I first got a glimpse of my father standing in line to greet us. He was staring at me from all angles, and when our eyes met he winked at me; it was a sweet, sweet wink. Just in that moment when our eyes met, I forgave my father for all the pain and hurt he had caused. He silently understood my gesture and nodded. That day when my father approached Anthony and me standing together with Anthony's hand across my waist, he was a different man. He looked straight into my eyes, then Anthony's. His eyes gleamed with pride; he reached out his hand for Anthony's, the two shook hands, then hugged, and my father approached me in a respectful manner and hugged me tenderly. He told me how happy I made him, he said his little girl was now a woman, she looked radiant, and he said he loved me. Yes my father told me he loved me. I think that was the only time I remember him saying so many tender words all at once to me – on my wedding day. It was also the first time I saw deep tenderness in his dark hurting eyes. That September day, if being married wasn't enough, having my father's blessings added more icing upon our cake. While my mother was still mourning the loss of her husband, my stepfather who could not be there to walk me up the aisle, that September day despite all the pain and hurt he was responsible for over many years, my father made me happy.

Chapter 15

Miguel Gabriel, 5 lbs. 14 ounces

"Push! Push!" Nurse Mark's voice echoed.

"Breathe Sue-Ann to my count," Dr. Achong-Low chimed in "1-2-3- push! One more time! Push!" Then, "Congratulations, you have a baby boy!" With Nurse Mark standing close by, Dr. Achong-Low pulled the baby out of my stretched vagina. His tone was rather surprising. He smiled, "Only the afterbirth left, no problem," he whispered. Having the baby was hard work, but *was that all?* I wondered to myself after months of hearing many gruelling accounts of childbirth that lasted more than twenty-four hours, caesarean section, and overbearing pain after delivery. Standing close by, my mother and husband kissed me. Dr. Low noted the date, Monday September 30, 1987, five pounds fourteen ounces, and the time 7:21pm.

The excitement and commotion of bearing my son quickly subsided. By the time I was wheeled into delivery, the nurses called Dr. Low who hurriedly rushed into the room. He stood over me, and assured me everything was OK. He told me we were ready to have the baby, and asked whether I was. He explained what he wanted me to do since much of the work was already done. They could have seen my son's head pushing its way out into the world. Dr. Low slowed my breath; he took my hand. I breathed in deeply, and pushed hard. On the second push the baby's head just slipped out, followed by a bloody and messy delicate body. Then, taking in his first breaths of life, he screamed; his voice brought joy to my heart and soul, the kind I could never have imagined. My mother and husband shared in the mystery of birth with awe and excitement. At that moment, all I could think about was my grandmother's words of wisdom;

"If you do everything I tell you, that baby will slip out of your womb with no problem whatsoever. The doctor and everybody will be amazed!"

During the pregnancy my grandmother cooked special dishes for me. She made me eat a lot of *ochroes*, stew with *ochroes*; steamed vegetables with *ochroes*; *ochroes* in soup; pumpkin, spinach and other vegetables always mixed with *ochroes*. She concocted home-made juices with soursop, mango, pineapple, and oranges; she made special baked desserts for me. She rubbed my belly and feet several times, mostly with coconut oil. Whenever I had a pain or complained, she listened and then whipped up something for me to drink adding many natural ingredients such as ginger, cinnamon and bay leaf.

After work time I tried doing chores around the house, cooking and cleaning. I became fatigued and weary, living on ginger ale and dry crackers for weeks, not daring to eat more solid and nourishing food. But my grandmother took good care of me. That's another reason why from a young age, I respected older people, especially women, for I believed they held many secrets. Many of them in my family were not willing to pass on this knowledge unless they really liked you, or to be more specific, if you took the time to visit with them, tweeze their graying hair, or ran errands for them; well maybe they'd talk with you, and give you some advice about life.

I don't know why I packed a bottle of red nail polish, nail polish remover, lipstick and make-up before leaving for the nursing home. My mother laughed when she unpacked the items, and wondered where I believed I was going, "To have my baby!" I had mockingly replied. "Child it's not a beauty parlor!"

"So what?" was my nervous reply. Making absolutely no sense, I further explained why I needed those things.

We arrived around noon at Amicus nursing home on Monday. It was only minutes away from our home. My Aunt Angela delivered her six children at the cozy Nursing home, and she assured us there was nothing to worry about. Nurse Mark was the best midwife; she'd take good care of me. Nursing home delivery and stay was expensive, but Anthony and I had carefully budgeted the expense. Anthony picked my mother and me up. I quit my job at Natalie's on Friday. Miguel was born on Monday. My bosses Mr. and Mrs. Williams gave me a small basket filled with baby items and delicate clothing. Once we arrived at Amicus I noticed the reception area was buzzing with pregnant women, younger children, and husbands waiting to register their wives, then to be escorted to their rooms. The atmosphere was warm, calm and friendly; several pictures of happy mothers holding healthy delivered babies, hung from pastel coloured walls.

We quickly settled into my room. The enema I was given was new and hot. I never had anything like that before. I never knew there was so much waste to let out before delivering a baby. In no time I rushed to the bathroom, with my mother and husband laughing, my mother saying, "And you want to play you're a woman, and have a child! Well all that is in it!" As advised by my doctor Anthony had already shaved me. Labor was induced. Nurses had instructions to call Dr. Low when it was time. Nurse Mark put the I.V. Catheter into my hand for the Saline drip, while I lay on the bed drifting in and out sleep, resting, with my family beside me talking, and keeping me calm, telling me this was the easy part. They were amused by the fact I was lying helplessly on the bed, vulnerable. My mother told Anthony stories about the day I was born, Christmas Eve, and what a busy day it was, how everyone was rushing around preparing for Christmas, making last minute trips to the stores, shopping, forgetting she might have the baby at any moment.

Sometime close to 6pm the pain intensified, I was breathing hard, screaming loudly and automatically pushing. My mother called the nurse. Without actually checking on me, one of the nurses remarked:

"She's not ready to deliver yet. She'll be spending the night with us. This is her first one, right?"

"Yes!" my mother replied.

But lying there on the bed something was happening fast…

I knew the baby was coming, I could feel it. I yelled again and again. My mother rushed once more to the nurse's station. By the time the nurse took one look between my legs she shouted, "Get the doctor. You know the little girl lying there on the bed, and having the baby easy like that!"

It was one of the most fulfilling experiences of my life. To trace each step of my son's birth until the day he was brought by a pair of wonderful hands, into this world has been my greatest joy. We had been married for about six months when Anthony and I visited my Aunt Angela one evening after work. One look at me, she asked whether I was OK. I mentioned to her I was not feeling well. It was only when my Aunt suggested I should make a doctor's appointment, that it occurred to me I might be pregnant. She, having borne six children, should know, I summed up after visiting with her doctor, Dr. Achong-Low when he confirmed her suspicions. The moment the doctor and I met there was good vibes from the small framed Chinese Trinidadian man. He was soft spoken and gentle. He was also the first doctor in Trinidad to successfully deliver Siamese twins. Dr. Achong-Low briefed me about my condition, pulled out his calendar, and slotted some dates in for future visits. He asked whether I was happy, while taking my medical history down. Dr. Achong-Low said I was about twelve weeks pregnant.

By the time news of my pregnancy got around, everyone in our family was excited: my mother's first grandchild; my grandmother's first great-grandchild; my sister's and brother's first nephew. The first few months of pregnancy were tough. I was sick for most of the day, not eating, feeling upset, and wanting to faint. Everyone said it will pass, but it seemed like a long time. I missed many days of work, and eventually my boss became impatient. He didn't pressure me or anything, but I suppose it was my own guilt playing tricks with me. With such feelings of sickness I often wondered whether I could have a child, or whether I was too sick to have a healthy baby. I didn't know the experience was part of the process of being pregnant. At the time I was working for Colibri Jewelers as a Junior Accounts clerk, working under an efficient and hard-working older woman named Lurline Sebro.

This was how I left my good job at Colibri. Anthony and I were engaged, to be married in one year. Only months before our wedding, one afternoon my boss called me into his office; we sat on his sofa, and were discussing staff placements for the five jewellery stores they owned which were located in Malls across the country. We were discussing who we would send to which shop, how we would alternate staff on weekends to ensure all hours were covered. I can't say what exactly happened to my boss, but in one moment we were talking, and in another he reached over, and grabbed for my breasts. I was in disbelief! I moved away, and as he started explaining himself in a way that made me feel sick, and then at the same time started an apology, I ran out of his office with tears streaming down my face. Then and there decided I would leave my job. Later, when I was a bit calmer, I relayed the incident to my supervisor, Lurline, who warned me not to tell my fiancé – that some things you don't tell men is what she said, Anthony might get the wrong message. *Why would Anthony get the wrong message? Would he think I led my boss on? That it was my fault and I wanted to be sexually harassed by my boss?*

That afternoon there were not many people in the office, my

boss's secretary was not present either. Lurline told me we should not let her know. Why? Because she would have great difficulty believing me, she trusted and believed in our boss too much. There was no doubt, Lurline believed me. She even told me she heard several reports he had done this before. At work things could never be the same for me. My boss kept his distance. Whenever he came out of his office, he didn't look my way. He went about his business ignoring my presence in the office. I suppose if I had given in to his demand that afternoon things at work would have been quite different for both of us. I would have been comfortable at work, and he would have had an assistant catering to his sexual whims and fancies after work. But I didn't, and so working at the office became awkward for him, and impossible for me. From the incident, I often wondered *why would a good man slip into such uncontrollable weakness and risk losing his own good reputation?*

Months later, we weren't surprised when our boss hired a new young woman to work at our office. She was friendly and lovely looking, eventually spending late evenings at work with the boss. We were even asked to train her, and show her exactly what our tasks were. During the day she frequented his office while I passed some of my duties to her. While one of my coworkers expressed disgust at the situation; we were just four women upstairs in the office, the new employee made five; she was obviously hired to replace someone. Not long afterward, the new employee was given a company car to drive; our boss claimed she would be on the road often doing company business. I started to figure out my boss didn't want me working for him anymore, and though he never said it to me, I knew from my own sense of job experience.

My boss attended our wedding as did many of my coworkers. Months after our wedding, and by the time I realized I was pregnant, and told my boss I saw his disappointment. I suppose he was thinking about having to pay me a salary while I was on maternity leave, and why would he want to do that? After all, I had not given in to his maddening sexual desire that afternoon, and he had already hired my replacement. He had already moved on, hired his own office girl, and was apparently quite happy with his wife not having a clue about the situation. I started to make my own plans for leaving the job, and since I was also ill, tendered my resignation just a few months into the pregnancy.

This experience was demeaning, it was my own first hand experience of sexual harassment on the job, and it was not pleasant. There was nothing I could have done. Who was there for me? Who would believe me when I observed many people protected those who did wrong things. What my boss did was wrong, but I lived and worked within a system that took such job related incidents as a big joke, usually blaming the woman. No one had the backbone to approach the wrongdoer. Unlike most of my other job situations, for a long time the experience left a bad taste in my mouth.

Anthony and I lived on Chow Quan Avenue, off Diego Martin Main Road after Miguel was born. It was a really nice comfortable two bedroom apartment, and we were content. After Colibri, I had later taken a job at Natalie's boutique in West Mall for a few months during the pregnancy, only because I was bored at home. The job offered flexible hours. I managed the shop during the day until the owners, who designed their own clothing for the store came in the afternoon. There was not much work to be done; I was alone during the day. It kept me busy, taught me more responsibility while I also had an income. I was accountable to my bosses, wrote reports, checked stock and balanced cash. I worked at Natalie's until the weekend before my son was born in September 1987. After becoming a mother, I left Natalie's to take care of my newborn.

We were a happy couple, now with a splendid addition to our family: a boy. There was some difficulty though in naming our son. From the start I wanted the name Antonio, named after his father Anthony. For some reason his father didn't like the name Antonio. Then there was the name Miguel, everyone wondered why we kept on choosing a Spanish name. As it turned out, my sister and I became friends at school with a boy from Venezuela whose name was Miguel. Since our meeting, and growing up, the name stuck with me. After running through lists of suggestions that lasted for about one month Michael Gabriel, Sean, Miguel, Antonio, we decided on Miguel, Gabriel. His grandfather, Anthony's father gave him the Christian name Gabriel as in Angel Gabriel who was born on the same day.

The experience of being a parent was new. My mother warned us we had to ask a question whenever we didn't know something. She said some things will come naturally, but we had to learn as we went along. She stayed with us for about one month after Miguel's birth. She helped wash her grandson's clothes. I loved to stand and watch washed white cotton diapers hanging on the line, catching sunlight, and delicate socks, booties, vests and blankets clipped with colored pins. My mother cooked and cleaned, while I breastfed my son and rested. There were restless nights, teary nights, and some lost nights from over-exhaustion. When my mother left us alone and returned to her home in Tobago, I didn't know whether I could be a good mother. Miguel was delicate and beautiful, always needing special care. We were constantly on the phone, asking about belly gripes, colds and fever. There was always someone, some family member especially my Aunt Angela, to give us advice and help us through the parenting process.

One weekend when we visited my grandmother, I remember she looked at me sternly and summoned me to the kitchen. I could not tell what was bothering her. Once alone with her, she asked me where was my make-up, and lipstick? Why hadn't I taken much care and attention with myself as I usually did? She told me I needed a hair cut, and some new clothes – that I looked plain. Yes that was the word she used "plain". In the cozy of our kitchen my grandmother warned me to keep myself looking beautiful – that my husband's eyes might fall somewhere else if I didn't pay attention to myself. She told me she hoped I was giving my husband sex otherwise he would look for it somewhere else. In one brief moment, my grandmother warned me about all these things and more.

My grandmother had me thinking about things I never considered. I became so wrapped up in caring for our son, not working, being a housewife that I forgot how it used to be before the baby. It wasn't so much that I forgot as much as it was how busy I'd become, how much loving, care and attention a baby needed. I wanted so much to be the perfect mother for our son I'd forgotten about being the perfect wife. But I promised my grandmother to take more care of my personal appearance. In time I knew she would also be the first to notice.

Chapter 16

Thinking of America

"The universe will reward you for taking risks on its behalf."

Shakti Gawain

Do you know where you're going to? Do you like the things that life is showing you? What are you hoping for? Where are you going to, do you know? The lyrics to Diana Ross' "Theme from Mahogany" were the same ones we sang twenty-five years ago at our school graduation. In many ways those lyrics formed the core of my life, as I have constantly asked myself the same questions. Back then still innocent, I had little knowledge about where those words would lead me.

As time progressed, it seemed I've carefully carried them within my bosom. For as far as I can remember, I have questioned life and the decisions I've made. *Was I happy? How happy? How much was I willing to pay for more happiness? Did I know I was going to America – that America was the place where I'd supposedly discover some of the things in life I had been looking for – that America was the place I'd unleash the very best of what had laid hidden from the world?* No! Not in my wildest imaginations. I always thought of America as a brutally harsh land. The place where pages of its history, as I'd often seen glorified on television, needed to be wiped clean from the history books! But indeed, it was in America I gained knowledge of some of the most significant lessons in life: I very quickly understood I didn't have to go in the same direction as the rest of the world, that I always had a choice, and that in my own particular way, I had the chance to make my own history – that while I could not change the world, I could change what I thought of it, and more importantly, I could always change me. It was the kind of realisation that hit hard. I realised no one out there could do for me what I wanted to do with my life presented me with the stark reality of my aloneness. It was from there I began to invest in me, most times, at a price that, in many ways, was still too high. Once you decide to become a writer, there is a responsibility attached to the title that is based on your truth.

My mother, Miguel, and I visited my sister in the USA, before his 1st birthday. Susan had been living in the USA about one year, having migrated in 1986. She lived in a place called Staten Island which was a twenty minute ride on a ferry from Manhattan. The island was cut off from the other boroughs: Brooklyn, Bronx, and Queens. For a while since Miguel's birth she had anticipated our visit; she was eager to meet her nephew. We didn't get Miguel his own Trinidad and Tobago passport because he was a minor, travelling with his mother, and so he could be endorsed on my passport. However, in order to travel to the USA, he had to obtain his own visa. At the time in the 1980s this process was not such a difficult one, at least not for us. Since I had travelled to the USA before, I already had a visa of my own. As a matter of fact one of my boss's wife worked at the US Embassy. When we discovered at the last minute he needed one, we sought her kind assistance. I considered myself lucky because while many people complained about being turned down at the US Embassy for no good reason, we got what we needed. At the time of my application I had a steady job, was married, and had a personal bank account. During the interview, I told the US Immigration officer I would never leave my homeland to live in the USA, that Trinidad was home for my family and me. It was the truth. According to American officials, chances were I would *only* visit America, not stay. My mother also wanted to visit with my sister; she didn't have a visa problem either; a few years before, the US Embassy had granted her a ten-year visa. All visas were gotten.

Once in the USA, and during the week, my sister worked on Staten Island, and she spent weekends with Aunt Theresa, my Uncle Lincoln's wife who had walked out on him. She lived in Brooklyn on Nostrand Avenue. During our visit, we also stayed with our aunt. My sister called everyday from her job on Staten Island telling us how she was doing, encouraging us to get out of the apartment, convincing us it was safe to take Miguel for a walk at the Botanical Gardens or just get something to eat. We eventually planned visits to the Bronx zoo, Gardens, Empire State, and took rides on the Staten Island Ferry, hung out at Battery City Park, and often visited the World Trade Center, which was conveniently located, and easily accessible from the subway. There were many shops, banks, a bookstore, and various eateries. We were visitors to the "Big Apple," and did things tourists did to entertain themselves. We took trips in the daytime, shopped, and made ourselves nuisances around the city, taking pictures everywhere we went.

For the month we visited in New York, I couldn't get accustomed to living in Brooklyn; it was overcrowded, people seemed to be living one on top of the other. Apartments were huge buildings; some elevators were often cramped and stuffy, or large and dingy with broken doors, and worse walls were scrawled with profanities. Although there were many people of Caribbean heritage living in the area, everyone was a stranger. It didn't seem safe talking with strangers inside large unfamiliar buildings. Observing things such as how my aunt shopped with a wire made push cart or did laundry using the same machines everyone else used was new to me, and at the same time, odd. People at Laundromats were not often friendly... or even considerate, shoving someone's wet clothes in open baskets without warning, rushing about for dryers or using more than two dryers at the same time.

Shopping at the Chinese markets for fresh fruits and vegetables was interesting because I easily recognised provisions, greens, dasheen bush, blue crab, bright yellow pumpkin, *ochroes*, and hot peppers. There you could also buy pigtail, salt fish, and other goods not usually sold in supermarkets. Even if I had a headache we could purchase a bottle of Alcolado Glacier or Limacol which instantly soothes hot aching heads. Whenever you asked for an item that was not stocked at the market, the Chinese merchants always tried to make it available on the next visit. Most everything we bought in our homeland could be found at Chinese markets. Chinese people knew how to make business prosper. I especially admired the fact they were always open, sometimes 24-7, could be seen stocking shelves late into the night, and before more Mexicans were hired, they also worked alongside their families.

Susan became close to the American family for whom she worked, and they even invited us over to Staten Island for dinner. On the weekend my sister always had something planned. We took the bus to the movies at Travis, visited friends in Connecticut or she prepared dinner. She loved to cook, and was happy preparing our meals. On one such occasion when my sister prepared a lovely dinner, she first planted the idea in my head of my leaving Trinidad to settle in the USA. Susan confided how much she missed her family, especially Miguel and I. She asked me whether without deciding anything I could just think about leaving Trinidad, and consider making a new life here in the USA. She said her employers would sponsor her for her green card, and she would then help us to settle down; she suggested we could get an apartment together. She assured my husband, Anthony he would be able to find a new job since he was a copy technician, he was skilled; skilled workers were always needed in the USA. I could baby-sit until I obtained work authorization. My initial response to this was surprise, followed by slight excitement at the thought of living in the USA. While I never pictured leaving Trinidad, the prospect of trying something new appealed in some way to my sense of adventure. That night without considering long term benefits or even disadvantages I told my sister I would think about starting a life in the USA, but would prefer her not mentioning the subject to my husband. I didn't say a word to him, at least not for another year.

After that conversation with my sister about leaving Trinidad and considering living in the USA I saw things differently, daydreaming on my own about what kind of life we might have in the USA. I didn't know where to start, how to begin or with whom I should even talk. You just don't return home after a vacation in the USA, and start talking about leaving Trinidad. And besides, I had some of my own judgments about America, "the land of milk and honey". I always considered it a rough place, the place where many history pages were unforgivable. Growing up in Trinidad watching glamorised versions about how the West was won always sickened me to my stomach. I watched Western movies, slave stories, and cried uncontrollably until I became too upset to think. I saw images of Native American Indians being murdered, fooled, robbed, treated as if they were nothing by the white man, their land taken away, their wives and women degraded, some ridiculed not to mention raped – I internalised such images. I believed America had *only* crazy white people who believed they owned the world, acted as such, and didn't care or even respected anyone who was not white American. Growing up, I also saw movies on slavery and hated white people even more. After all, these were descendants of those who went before; could you really expect more from them? What kind of people would treat another human being in such inhumane ways, and decades later arrogantly boast about their history of freedom and democracy? I was certain Americans didn't have a religion, or culture of their own so they had to steal everyone's, and then lament about all they had taken away. *So why would I even think about leaving the warmth of Trinidad where my family loved me, where I had a life of my own, a good paying job, why would I leave this comfort zone to settle for something I was not a part of? We were accustomed to living in our own family homes in Trinidad where we didn't rent but instead owned our own homes. Even after marriage, once agreed upon, you could remain in your family home, work and save enough to build or purchase your own home. It was the place where the ocean was warm, soothing and inviting... just minutes away as opposed to cold and contaminated... home was the place where all our worries were taken care of by family... Trinidad...; it was my home. We had carnival and Indian culture.* Over months those thoughts were only a few that quietly taunted me. While I knew several people who migrated to the USA and visited us occasionally, there was no one with whom I could openly talk about my fears.

Months later my sister called us in Trinidad, and reminded me of all we had discussed. I told her the picture was already painted in my mind, and I would let her know. My sister became persistent, and at the same time our living situation in Trinidad was becoming harder. In the two years since our marriage we had moved three times. After living with my in-laws for about three months, we started looking for an apartment, and found one in La Horquette, Glencoe. This was up scale, the rent was $1000 but we decided to move anyway. We lived there about eight months, just before giving birth to our son. We had to find something less expensive because of the expenses that came with a baby. We found and moved to a small neighbourhood in Diego Martin, paying a monthly rent of $850. It was a small cozy two bedroom, but while neither Anthony nor I was comfortable with the fact our landlord lived next door, we stayed. Every time we knocked the wall to hang a picture, the landlord would come over to see what we were doing. If we had friends over, they had to leave by a certain time since "they" were early sleepers, and after all it was their building. The mistake we made was moving too quickly from my in-laws home. But you don't realise it is a mistake until it is made.

Quite unexpectedly, one day my Uncle Lincoln called, and asked to speak with us. Lincoln told us he was going to America to live with his wife, Theresa, and daughter Sandra who had left years earlier when Sandy was five. His wife promised to file resident papers for him to live in the USA. He asked us whether we would live in his place, the same one he built, and had lived there alone since his wife and daughter left in late 1970s. This self-contained apartment was downstairs from my grandmother's, the same place I grew up. It was a God sent offer, and without much hesitation we accepted. Weeks later our family moved from Chow Quan Avenue to Crystal Stream much to my grandmother's and uncles' delight. Not only was I returning home, but I also brought along a husband and a son. I was close to my family, just downstairs. Both Anthony and Miguel would have the chance to benefit from the same love and gentle care that nurtured me into adulthood.

Miguel loved Ninja, the dog my uncle left behind. He ate everything, and without us knowing, also fed Ninja whatever he was eating. It was only when I caught the little toddler licking his chicken bone, afterward putting it into the dog's mouth to lick, and then he put it once again into his own mouth that I realised what he had been doing. I saw this from a distance in the kitchen while Miguel had been sitting on the steps eating the chicken drumstick. When I angrily yelled "Miguel, don't!" he burst out screaming, startled by the stern sound of my voice. Of course the incident became a cute growing up joke.

Marinating for months on the topic of moving to America, just when I was bursting at the seams, I first told someone, my mother. She had been visiting us in Trinidad. We all went with Aunt Angela and visited with my mother's first cousin, Claudette. My mother, Aunt Angela, Miguel and I visited with Claudette. At Claudette's home in Petit Valley, we discussed the matter of us leaving for America. My mother told me to follow my heart – that I always knew what I was about, and she would support any decision I made. Claudette gave me many positive things to think about; she was well travelled and had friends and family leave Trinidad to live abroad. She said it would not be easy, settling somewhere strange never is. My Aunt Angela smiled quietly acknowledging all that was said, but her eyes were filled with tears and pain at the thought of us leaving home.

After that conversation, the next step, the hardest step would be convincing Anthony we could start a new life in a foreign land. It wasn't going to be an easy task; he was steady, and for the most part, set in his ways. But he loved his family, and eventually when he agreed to the plan, I believe it was only for me that he agreed, not that he wanted to leave Trinidad, but because he could not think of living without me, and most especially without his son. I came to understand when women gathered together it was to talk about important things. Women in our family talked whenever there was a need to talk. They usually got together to talk, eventually coming to a reasonable decision for the greater good of their family. Those three ladies, my Aunt Angela, Cousin Claudette, and my mother were important people in our family; they weighed situations and gave advice. In this way they showed love and support. I felt I was important: I was married, had a son, had a job and savings, and was on the verge of making another big decision. In their eyes I was a woman; at twenty-six, I was making womanly choices and taking chances without knowing the outcome of such chances. I was finally becoming my own woman.

Weeks later, Anthony came home from work to find me listing all the items in our apartment, taping prices to the items. When he asked what I was doing, I immediately told him we were having a garage sale to get some money to travel abroad. Though he looked at me as though I was a crazy person; I continued listing items, unopened wedding gifts, household appliances, and things. The garage sale went on for more than one month; we put an advertisement in the local newspapers and also called family and friends. We sold almost everything we had, crystals, book shelves, corning dishes in white, matching cutlery, exercise equipment, and other household items. We made a lot of money, thousands paid in cash. Anthony was becoming anxious, things were happening fast, he didn't know whether this was the right decision. I assured him it was. I am still not sure what actually lured me to America, but deep inside I was convinced the desire to try something new was a big a part of my restless nature – my hunger to live and experience new things – even not knowing how it would turn out, the uncertainty never bothered me as much as it did Anthony. Moving ahead to a distant land, a harsh land I might later learn to call home inspired me.

Slowly months passed and the reality of what we were doing became more apparent; some family expressed opposing views. Anthony's older sister in particular wasn't too keen with our leaving. While she was married, had her own family including two children, and lived with her parents, she couldn't see we had to make our own life, whether we chose to live in Trinidad or somewhere else. She was always over protective of her brother, could not let go of the fact he was married, and he had to put his own family first. I eventually told her all she could do was be happy for us since the decision was already made, and we were moving forward with our plans. From early she knew I was mainly responsible for our sudden move to the USA. She eventually accepted.

After Miguel was born, I accepted a new job at the Princess Elizabeth Center for the Handicapped as Administrative Assistant to the Manager of Gokool's Workshop. This was another job where I worked among men. In fact, at Gokool's I was the only woman working among four men. The workshop was an annexed building to the Center, the place where young children were fitted with orthopedic shoes, and also young girls who were suffering from scoliosis came in for braces. At the workshop I learnt mostly teenage school girls suffered from this curvature of the spine which was mainly caused because they carried heavy book bags before backpacks, placing immense weight upon the shoulder. Over time this bad habit placed the spine out of alignment to the degree of it becoming curved. Worse cases occurred when shoulders protruded out of alignment. At the shop three skilled staff personnel made braces for the young girls, who were first measured and fitted. The brace was an uncomfortable thing to wear underneath school uniforms, but it promised relief, and an eventual straightening out of the spine. Over months I saw improvement in some clients and young girls spoke about feeling relieved of the back pain caused as a result of the physical damage to the spine.

I was saddened when I tendered my resignation from the Workshop; I would miss lunch time visits to the Center, talking with handicapped children, distributing lunches, walking with them in the warm sunlight, reading stories under shady trees, and watching them laugh, if only for brief moments. I would miss this job most. I would miss the warm people with whom I worked. We had become our own family. Anthony had already handed in his resignation at Pereira's; his bosses begged him to reconsider. He carried the weight of our leaving. While I worked and changed several jobs over the six years of our being together, his job remained constant, his friends, and what he was leaving behind a reminder of his deep loyalty.

It was mid September 1989 when we left Trinidad. Miguel was only weeks away from turning two. The hardest thing I had yet to face was leaving my grandmother behind. She stood close to the stairs wiping away tears; although she told me she would be fine and understood why we were leaving. I knew we had just broken her heart into several pieces, the weight of which she would carry for many years.

Chapter 17

First Impressions, Second Home

"I am not afraid of storms, for I am learning how
to sail my ship."

Louisa May Alcott

It is a rainy morning in New York City. From the subway to the office, I don't open the worn out umbrella I'm carrying even while light drops of rain hit hard on my face, cold and fresh. Walking along wet streets, I reminisce about rainy days in Trinidad, lying upon the warm bed beside my grandmother curling my legs into hers, while listening to heavy showers beat on galvanised roofs, hearing water pouring heavily filling the concrete drain in our backyard where some serious boating events took place inside the drain, with us running from one yard to the next following cardboard boats down swift water, down to where we yanked our boats out before the small drain emptied into the larger canal heading towards the river.

Sometimes boats were made out of small pieces of wood, a test to determine which was stronger. Often in a burst of excitement I would dress in T-shirt and cotton shorts, and run out into the backyard. I would stand in pouring rain or run about the slippery dirt yard. Looking towards the kitchen I'd hear my grandmother shouting, "Yuh better come back inside, you know how you quick to start sneezing and catch a cold!" I'd giggle. With rain water filling my mouth, I'd answer, "Tina don't worry yourself, everything is fine!" Then I'd gargle cold water and spit. After being drenched and loving the way wet clothes clung to my scrawny body, with all my fingers and toes curled, lips trembling and body shaking as if in a trance, I'd quietly crawl up the back steps towards the bathroom.

There I would stare at the dripping bony figure staring back at me in the long old-fashioned brass mirror. I would watch how my straight black hair stuck to my scalp, neck and back, and how the bangs on my forehead still dripped down my face. I would try to lick drops of water trickling down my face past the corners of my mouth. With water still running off soaked clothing, I would stand and admire the sight of growing breasts, printed plain through wet T-shirt, how they would stand out, cold and firm, nipples pointed. Embarrassed, I darted under a cold shower to prolong my vain pleasure.

When we landed at JFK International, Anthony and I were uncertain about what the future held in store for us. My mother had suggested we leave Miguel in Trinidad with her; she would look after him until we settled down, and could afford to send for him. From the start, the idea of leaving our son behind in search of "a better life" for ourselves was impossible for me. As a mother, I could not see myself leaving my first son, and only child behind. I'd heard too many sad stories about children being separated from their parents because they left them behind, and intended to send for them, which sometimes didn't happen for years, I decided wherever we chose to live that's where our son would live.

The bigger picture of taking our son away from his home to live in a foreign land had not yet struck us. It would take years for that reality to hit home. The airport was large and spacious. Though I travelled through it before, it was not familiar. With its long corridors, high ceilings, and frightening quiet, this time in some odd way it reminded me of the police station I visited as a child in Trinidad. I suppose because I knew we were going to stay in the USA the surroundings affected me differently. There were definite restrictions; uniformed officers were stationed at various points through which everyone had to pass in order to get beyond those boundaries. With little noise, people were hustling back and forth, filling out forms, whispering, and standing in queues. Americans were the only people who walked fastest through the airport terminal and after lining up were on their way in only a matter of minutes. They went directly to lines with green arrows pointing towards signs "US Citizens." Their lines moved more quickly with USA officials barely looking up. All we heard was the push down click of some kind of metal stamp upon the counter. From early, I noticed Americans had privileges. When we approached the USA Immigration officer together he asked us why we came to the USA .We told him we were visiting my sister and aunt with whom we would be staying, and gave him their address. Wishing us a happy visit to the USA he stamped our passports for a six-month stay in the United States, for which we had to eventually apply for extensions.

The fall was a beautiful season; I remember varying colours of leaves changing oranges to reds, mingling brown leaves, and soothing winds during Indian summers, and mind provoking sunsets. Summer days in New York were much different from Trinidad where it was summer all year long. New Yorkers looked forward to warmer days, when temperatures soared; they lived for the change of seasons, and seemed to have a contagious appreciation for warm days. We would see many seasons change; it was new and exciting – something to look forward to.

In one week after our arrival Miguel turned two; we had a birthday party for him at our aunt's place in Brooklyn. A few friends, including my cousin Sandra and her mother, my Uncle Lincoln's wife, Theresa, who left Trinidad years before, were present. They brought along some friends. Miguel had the chance to cut his birthday cake with one of their friend's daughter who was barely two. It was a beautiful sight when our son bent over to kiss the toddler right upon her lips. Everyone laughed hysterically.

In the weeks that followed we unpacked, slowly trying to calm the doubts and fears we were both having. We lived in Brooklyn on St John's at Eastern Parkway, close to the Brooklyn Museum; my mother had asked a distant relative, her first cousin on her mother's side, named Horace to have us stay at their home. We came to know them as Auntie Jane and Uncle Horace. Auntie Jane was from Santo Domingo, and was a nurse. They were both retired USA citizens having already paid their dues to their adopted home. Auntie and uncle made us feel welcome, gave us their second bedroom, and told us we could stay as long as we liked. They related stories about when they first came to the USA, and started their own life, how difficult it was, how many times they wanted to return to their home country. But they told us while making immense sacrifices they managed to stay together, and have a comfortable life.

They were glad to have Miguel and loved him dearly. He brought excitement to their mundane days. Auntie cooked him special dishes; he loved her spaghetti and meatballs, Spanish style, and chicken. She bought him gifts, toys and things, anything she wanted to buy him. Since they had no children of their own, our son brightened their otherwise lonely life in Brooklyn, and they quickly grew a close attachment to him. They especially loved to take him for long afternoon walks at the Botanical gardens, putting on his baseball cap and jeans jacket, while carefully watching the toddler run around and have fun with other kids.

Settling into a bedroom, living with my mother's relative and his wife who we hardly knew was not our idea of going the USA to start our own life. But we were aware of this before leaving Trinidad; we knew what we had to do, except when the reality hit us, it was quite another story. Both Auntie and Uncle were there for us, trying to make us comfortable. Auntie had a strong Spanish accent, but also spoke English fluently. Uncle usually sat at the window in a single chair looking towards the street. From there he talked, watched mostly sports and news, drank beer, and sometimes ate. Auntie always yelled at him telling him no more beer. But he paid her no mind, and usually did his own thing.

We shopped for warm clothes. Auntie took us around to get bargains and some of the things we needed immediately. She told us the first season would be our most expensive; she was right. We spent hundreds on winter coats and accessories for three. We bought boots and sneakers, gloves, hats and scarves. Auntie gave me a few pieces of clothing she had for years, which fit me, but she wasn't a small woman so her coats and other things were oversized. There was no rush so we bought more clothing and essentials as we went along. We offered to give auntie and uncle some money each week for our stay, but they would not hear of it. They told us when we got jobs, we'll see, but first concentrate on employment and settling in. We immediately noticed that Auntie Jane shopped with plastic cards and did not pay any money. We were not accustomed to buying things and paying later. Once we tried to rent a car and our hard earned cash was refused for credit. We realised we had to create a credit history of our own and assimilate into the American way of spending.

With all the accommodation and hospitality from both Auntie Jane and Uncle Horace I was still used to having my own, and wanting my own life. In the quiet of my mind it bothered me that we had to depend on someone else to help us along. I was so independent and often wondered about how we inconvenienced both Auntie and Uncle. Sometimes at night when Auntie and Uncle quarreled mostly about uncle's drinking, and then she rattled off words in Spanish, and further got on the phone and spoke to her friends or relatives in Spanish, I was certain she talked about us, and our presence in their home. On such nights we remained in our bedroom and didn't come out until the next morning. The next day Auntie would be back to her usual self, assuring us their quarrel had nothing to do with us, and uncle would continually tell us not to mind her, "she's a crazy woman."

On the weekend my sister would come by. She would have some outing planned or together we visited friends. We spent some Sundays giving Auntie and Uncle their space while we went over to my cousin's Sandra and her mother's place between Nostrand and Sterling on Lefferts. They lived on the sixth floor. Whenever Te (Theresa) was off from work, she cooked lunch; we ate, and hung out. She loved playing music, taking Miguel in her arms and dancing with him all afternoon. She was a funny person, warm and easy to get along with. She was also a great cook, and joked around, saying we didn't feed the child because he ate her all food, even wanted more.

My favourite place was visiting the Bronx Zoo. We sometimes left Brooklyn at 10am having enough time to walk around and spend a fun day. We carried a food bag, change of clothing for Miguel, camera and other essentials. We visited the zoo whenever it was open and walked for miles enjoying Miguel's excitement when he saw the animals, monkeys, tigers, giraffes, and when the sea lions were fed fresh fish around 4pm each day. It was a sight; the seals clumsily jumped high into the air caught the fish, and happily danced into the water, then came up again for another round. My sister and I were close; she needed family close to her, and we leaned on her. She was good to us, and helped us during the time when settling in the USA seemed most difficult. She commuted from Staten Island each weekend to spend time with us, and left early Monday morning. Over time, our dependence on each other grew, and our sister-to-sister relationship blossomed into a deeper love and bond.

By Thanksgiving, two months after coming to the USA there was much we felt we were grateful for. First of all, we had somewhere to live; Auntie and Uncle were good to us; my sister was there for us, and it seemed our life was beginning again. That year there was a snowfall; Auntie said the first in many years on Thanksgiving. We put on our clothes, boots, socks, gloves, scarves, hats and coats, and took Miguel outside to enjoy our first snow play. It was awesome – the excitement of watching him not knowing what to do, the loud laughter of kids in the distance, the sky white and alive. Thanksgiving was a special time for Auntie as well as for many Americans. Auntie usually had a feast and invited many people, friends and family over to her home. The day before I had seen the huge frozen bird lying upon the kitchen counter, and then it disappeared. That Thanksgiving morning moments before we walked out the door, I saw the bird again, this time in a large baking pan. Auntie was happy and singing. She told us to go and have some fun outside.

Our first Thanksgiving dinner as a family in the USA was spent with another family. My sister and I helped Auntie in the kitchen, preparing dishes, cutting up vegetables, but Auntie had everything under control. She had been preparing for days. By the afternoon, we set the table and all sat to a wonderful home cooked dinner, with my sister, Auntie and Uncle making toasts and thanking us for being with them, telling us how happy we made them. Some friends and family randomly dropped in for dessert or just to say hello. It seemed everyone was already full from having shared lavish meals with their own family. Auntie played Latin music to which she danced and sang; she dressed up like many Spanish people do. Auntie Jane was a sexy dresser wearing broad matching hats, and off the shoulder dresses that silhouetted her full figure. Admiringly, my sister and I looked on. That first Thanksgiving in 1989 was the best we spent in the USA.

After Thanksgiving December quickly followed; it was also our first Christmas, and so everyone made it special for us. New

York City was a beautiful buzz of activity. Strings of lights, trees and ornaments decorated streets, homes and plazas. We found some favourite places to visit; among them were Fulton Street near the water, Rockefeller Center, Central Park and Little Italy. On afternoons or weekends we made trips to those places, had dinner, shopped or just walked around. I especially liked going to Little Italy for Italian desserts, my favourite being cannoli and éclairs and we washed the treats down with tea before cappuccinos. We walked through Canal Street, taking in sights, smells, and the curious lure of Chinese street vendors always stimulated my creative juices.

Things happened simultaneously on Canal Street as they did in Brooklyn; the two became cultural centres: Caribbean and Koreans in Brooklyn and those from Taiwan, Shanghai and other Eastern places monopolised China Town. Immigrants worked hard to make a living, taking care of themselves and their families; even sending money to their home country to help loved ones they left behind. It was their contribution having left their homeland. I believed this was the purpose of migration – to make better of one's living conditions, and then give something back to your homeland. People didn't come to the USA with the intention of taking away someone else's job; in fact they came here to do a job, which many Americans would not do such tasks as babysitting, taking care of the elderly and house cleaning. In the early seventies and even before that time, America advertised jobs in local newspapers luring Caribbean people to the USA, promising a successful future, permanent resident papers and citizenship. Many people took advantage of such opportunities, coming to the USA, leaving their good paying jobs, their homes and assets to settle for lives of uncertainty, often starting at the bottom of the work ladder. People from the Caribbean did not reduce the availability of American jobs; they filled a void: they worked hard at childcare, and cared for the elderly; nurses and teachers also sacrificed much to make a "better life." It didn't come for free either. Often US employers promised to file petitions on behalf of those they employed.

Sometimes they did; often they pretended they did, making your stay with them extended for years. There were no handouts; you had to pay your way every step of the journey. While a number of my friends left Trinidad and worked as housekeepers, eventually obtaining permanent resident status; many did not have a straightforward story to tell.

When you are an undocumented worker in the USA, you don't qualify for many privileges Americans enjoy. As a result you pay much more for services such as health care, and especially education. But you came to the USA with an intended purpose, so you learn to endure your circumstances. Immigrants have for many years paid a high and severe price for their unauthorised stay in the USA. For years their voices have been silenced because of the harshness of the law; they have endured much suffering. But they have struggled onward, hoping and waiting, and most of all, praying for the day when the law will see it fair to publicly acknowledge their contribution to the growing economy, and see it fit to make them legal residents with the promise of attaining American citizenship. In my own case, we were undocumented workers for a number of years until I obtained a work visa. This visa however only allowed me to work at the Consulate General for my home country. It limited opportunities for me in the USA. My husband waited on the opportunity for job sponsorship, a long process that took years; worse; no one was assured of final approval.

Christmas was not only wonderful; the day before Christmas was my birthday; my sister treated me to dinner before we attended midnight mass – just she and I. My sister took me to a cozy and expensive Italian restaurant on Staten Island; she treated me to a delicious dinner. We sipped expensive red wine, and I was delighted when the waiter put the dessert menu before me. Italian pastries were simply the best. On Christmas morning I remember thinking Christmas was really for children when I saw the look and gleam in our son's eyes the moment he glimpsed his first tricycle.

He had gotten trucks, cars, and several other toys, but nothing excited him more than the bright yellow and blue tricycle, my sister's gift to her nephew. Once more we had a nice family dinner with friends and family dropping by. On this occasion, my sister and I cooked, and we allowed Auntie Jane time out to relax all day.

The New Year came; the season changed and we were somewhat adjusted to our new lives. Months passed. Seasons changed. In September we attended the West Indian Labor Day celebrations in Brooklyn. There were thousands and thousands of people gathered along Brooklyn streets much like Carnival in Trinidad. But the crowd grew thicker and denser, and pretty soon we found ourselves swallowed by masses of people with a two-year-old baby. I felt suffocated, and in vain we tried several times to get out of the crowd. Eventually we did, having to walk blocks and blocks before finding ourselves to the subway. Eventually I grew weary of all the West Indian outings, gatherings and parties. I felt I didn't come to a foreign land to hang out with my own people all the time. I often became bored with their way of life in the big city.

As time passed I became immersed in American culture in a way many of my friends had not. I wanted to understand it. In fact, in many ways I saw myself becoming part of it, working hard each day, taking care of family needs, having some bigger dream, enjoying holidays, and visiting with some American friends I met on my adventures. The American way of life was also becoming a part of me, eating on the run, reading daily newspapers, and minding my own business. I wore suits to work. We had assimilated.

Chapter 18

Looking for a JOB in the Big "A"

"If life were predictable, it would cease to be life and be without flavour."

Eleanor Roosevelt

It was a lovely day. Bright sunshine and soothing breezes made my spirit warm and alive. I felt like dancing. Two friends and I carelessly wandered about several blocks along Second Avenue. We watched people, buildings, and things, commenting on expressions, outfits and men. I noticed how beautifully rays of sunlight slanted across taller buildings. We talked and stopped a few times to gaze through store windows that teased in the summer displaying skinny mannequins dressed in shorts and sexily cut, printed T-shirts. *Why do they advertise such skinny impressions of women, when full grown women seldom have legs as lean as those, well developed breasts, let alone waist measurements that are in many cases only suitable for dolls?* I questioned.

We talked about how women punish themselves to fit into advertised sizes and shapes, stilettos, and tight garments and about how much is demanded of women in respect of appearance. I mentioned the funny thing was that if a man was overweight, it seemed to go by unnoticed, but, whenever a woman put on a few extra pounds, she was considered overweight. My girlfriend agreed and said in America, obesity was a big problem – Americans watched too much TV, ate too many bags of potato chips, and were not active. We talked about the word "moderation," and how important it was to do a little of everything – to not over indulge in too much food, sex, exercise, in attaining wealth, status or worldly possessions. While it was important to stay on middle ground, it was equally significant to maintain flexibility, especially in making decisions about one's own life. We need to remember things in excess can become harmful to our well being, dulling our senses; making us into parasites, always wanting to suck up everything we can get from another person, and from life.

Settling in the USA was not easy. It was no vacation, and the reality of adjusting to life in a foreign land save for a few friends and family members quickly hit us hard. Home was some 3,000 miles away. I was naïve, just married to a handsome young man, and also responsible for our son. Wanting something more, I didn't know whether it could be found in the USA, but I was willing to try. From the beginning, even though I was prepared to babysit I never got a babysitting job. At least, not immediately. The only jobs readily available to most immigrants were babysitting and housekeeping, and while I was interviewed several times for such a job, I had no success. Most American husbands were willing to hire me. They saw me as friendly, smart, and especially because I was married and had a son of my own, also believed I was capable of caring for theirs. However, it was American wives who experienced most difficulty in employing me. They openly said I was overly confident which raised their suspicions, too smart, and didn't seem needy, and yes, they also said I was much too pretty. I don't know whether they even considered the possibility I needed a job, wanted a job, wanted to get my life started, and had to earn an income in order to help take care of our family needs. According to my sister, and her babysitting friends, perhaps those wives believed I would eventually become a distraction to their husbands, my sister and her friends consoled me by saying *they* were the insecure ones. Whatever their reasons were, I wasn't hired.

In a matter of months of our arrival to the USA my husband was hired as a copy technician in the hope of job sponsorship. He repaired and updated office copiers and fax machines. It was a period of adjustment for us both. He got the job working for a small company in mid town Manhattan. It was the same type of work he was accustomed to doing in Trinidad, and from that aspect, the job was familiar. But the working environment was much different. The adjustment took a longer time; in fact it took years. First he had to get accustomed to the language, English spoken with an American accent. This proved a little difficult, and needed more practice in listening than speaking. Americans spoke fast, and explained things in a straightforward manner.

Then there was weather conditions, which he quickly learned frequently changed. "Never leave the house without first listening to the weather!" we had been warned by several people. In Trinidad Anthony drove from one office to another, mostly in temperatures above 80 degrees. Here in New York he had to cope with the seasons, summer being the most uncomfortable for him since streets were overcrowded, and he had to get used to the heat and humidity underground which often became unbearable. In the spring he suffered from allergies.

Anthony walked from office to job carrying a large case with office tools, visiting companies that leased office copiers from their privately owned business. In many cases he took mass transit. During the day it was more of a hustle, travelling to and from each office, walking long blocks, dealing with impatient customers, missing lunch, and working late hours. As time passed he developed his own time schedule, changing in ways that matched his new working environment. He liked the cool of autumn, dressing only minimally, and became quite comfortable commuting back and forth. During winter months it was a new adjustment; icy cold winds, low temperatures and snow. Still, he had to walk from office to office braving harsh weather, storms and even blizzard conditions.

I remained at home with Miguel only for a short time, taking care of him. While everything was going well at Auntie and Uncle's home in Brooklyn, and no one pressured us to leave, I always wanted our own life. I yearned to live somewhere, just the three of us with my sister visiting with us on weekends. When we were first married we lived with Anthony's parents in Diamond Vale for three months. That was as much as I could take. Being newlyweds, I believed we should have been on our own, and again no one ever pressured us to move out. Having discussed the matter with Anthony he agreed we should aim to have our own place. On the weekend we started shopping around for household items and things we needed to furnish our own apartment. Since we left Trinidad and sold most of what we owned, we had to start again. This was not easy. If we needed a spoon, we had to buy a spoon. We were jolted into reality here in the USA. I knew it was a consequence of the choice we made to come to America. Whenever my sister got her weekly earnings, she gave me some money, sometimes $50 or $60 to begin buying things we might need later. My sister was not a shopper, actually she hated stores. She preferred to give you the money to get her whatever she needed. I was used to doing her shopping while she sat outside the store patiently waiting to see what I bought. With the money my sister gave me, I started stocking up on household items, making lists according to rooms under headings such as Things for Kitchen, Bedroom, Living room, Bath. Within a few months our bedroom was filled with shopping bags which were sorted and labelled.

We socialised with my sister's friends on some weekends, but by the time the season changed, it seemed everyone disappeared into long coats and lives of hibernation. Besides, early evenings were darker, and I realised there were more things we had to adjust to in the USA than we could have imagined. It wasn't just about trying to be understood when you said tomato (ma) instead of tomato (may); it was more about being understood in a good way. When the clock moved back, and there was an hour difference in daylight which was called daylight savings time, something as simple as that was hard to understand. *What was the relevance of that practice? Why did Americans need an extra hour?* Nevertheless, we had to fall in line with the pattern, having early dinners, watching movies and settling in for the night.

Time passed as we faced our lives in the USA. We didn't call home often because I was too lonely and every time I spoke with my grandmother it brought so many tears, memories and pain, I became sick for days. So Auntie suggested we not call too often, that we needed time to adjust ourselves. One day I wrapped my whole heart around my granny and hid her inside every corner of my body and mind. Whenever I needed her, it wasn't hard. That was how I survived living away from her. I tried to move on with our life, focusing on our new life in the USA, and became certain my granny was present everywhere I went.

One day a friend of a friend called and asked whether I was still looking for a job. She said she had a job, but had to leave for a few weeks, and her employers needed someone to hold on in her position for the time she was away. She wanted to know whether I would be interested, and mentioned I had to start immediately. I told her I was, but would have to talk with Anthony when he returned from work that day. She said she would call later that night. The moment I mentioned the job prospect to Anthony he was excited but cautioned me not to get my hopes up too high in case it didn't work out. Being the person I am I told him to watch and see how everything would work out. That night when our friend called, and I confirmed I was interested, and Anthony agreed; she gave me details about where to go, who to ask for, whose name to use, and all the things I needed to say. She told me I could travel into the city with Anthony.

Anthony dropped me at the door of 420 Lexington Avenue, on the third floor, the office of the Consulate General of the Republic of Trinidad and Tobago. He kissed me, wished me good luck, and walked away. He would pick me up later. I rang the door bell and was led in by a medium framed well dressed gentleman. He introduced himself as Mr. Learie Rousseau, Deputy Consul General, and led me to a small room where he told me to have a seat. He knew who I was and said a friendly hello. Not long afterwards, Mr. Rousseau led me to a large spacious office where I sat, and another man who introduced himself as Mr. Rambissoon, Consul General, approached his desk.

After asking a few questions back and forth to which I answered to his liking, Mr. Rousseau led me towards a smaller room with a typewriter, gave me a few sheets of paper and asked me to transcribe some notes and retype for him. I was shaking. At that time, while I could type fairly well, under pressure was another story. Mr. Rousseau assured me there was no rush, I could take my time. And so I did. I typed the document as he requested. He took one glance at the type written letter and said that was fine.

I followed Mr. Rousseau into the computer room where he enquired whether I had used one before. Luckily, thanks to my boss at Colibri, we had all been broken in to the computer world. That pleased Mr. Rousseau. At the time the programs I learnt were DOS and Word Perfect. Mr. Rousseau left me alone for a while, returning not long afterwards with a smile telling me I was hired for three to five weeks, and could start the next day if I wanted to. I said I would. I started work at the Consulate General's office for Trinidad and Tobago in the middle of the week; my weekly salary was $120.

Anthony and I celebrated over lunch in the city, and he was happy for me. In fact, he was also glad it was a familiar environment where only Trinidadians worked. He knew I could handle the job, and would not be uncomfortable. I was hired as a temporary clerical officer, filling in for someone on vacation, typing for more than one officer as requested, but working under Mr. Rousseau's supervision. As needed, I was called upon to function in another section of the office, Passports and Immigration. The office was not big, there was a receptionist, a security officer, an accounts department, made up of only one officer, a passport section made up about five people including a counter officer, and the Consul, Immigration, Administrative division with Consul General, Deputy Consul General, and one Administrative Secretary to both positions. Auntie and Uncle were happy for me, and assured me they would take care of Miguel during the day while we both worked.

I started working at the Consulate General's office in midtown, commuting to work, having to take one train #2 or #3 from Brooklyn to Nevins where I switched for the Lexington lines #4 or #5 which took me to Grand Central station. Starting off at work was exciting, and I had the gut feeling we were getting our life started – coming to the USA was a good choice after all. By the time news about my employment got to Trinidad everyone was also happy for me, my mother saying she knew I would eventually get a job. When I started work I was qualified with all my job training skills and experience; I knew office etiquette and was extremely self disciplined. But I also knew from the start the job was not permanent and so we kept asking around, trying to find something else for me when the three to five weeks were up. On the job, I was regular and punctual, pleasant and personable, always at my desk performing tasks assigned to me, getting along well with staff members. I worked as a receptionist, typed letters, performed clerical duties when staff was insufficient or on vacation. When I started work at the Consulate General's office while I was naïve about life in the big city of New York, I was no novice to the office environment. I was skilled, trained, could be depended upon to complete tasks, and loyal. After three weeks, the person who left on vacation sent a letter to have her time away extended for another three weeks. I was asked to hold on longer. In no time, I had adjusted nicely to my working routine, made a few friends at the office, and showed enough potential that when the person who I filled in for sent in her resignation after about seven weeks vacation, Mr. Rousseau called me into the office, and without hesitation officially offered me a job, which I gladly accepted.

From the beginning I liked my boss Mr. Rousseau; he was warm and friendly. He liked to talk and tell stories about his experiences working in government. I enjoyed listening to him since I had never worked in government, and had come from private enterprise. Working for private companies in Trinidad was much different from being employed with government. For one thing, there was more accountability. My boss was not a demanding boss; his personality drew his staff towards him in a good way. You could say most of the time he was a people's person. But this sometimes got in the way of him making firm decisions regarding staff and office procedures. I suppose he wanted to remain the nice guy believing he could manage an office and still remain friends with most people. The more I observed his approach to management the more I realised this was near impossible, given the fact that many people used his good natured spirit to take advantage of office protocol.

Commuting daily into the city was new, much unlike many trips we had casually taken during vacation or the weekend when trains were less crowded, clean and more bearable. Getting familiar with subway lines was a challenge; most times I ended up somewhere downtown when I should have been heading uptown. Having to ask strangers for directions was not always a good option since many people also didn't know their way around the city. Auntie had warned me over and over to only ask a policeman for directions because people can often mislead.

During the morning rush trains were jam packed; people squeezed themselves silly unto trains as if there were no more trains coming. Seeing this every morning I immediately imagined cans of sardines packed in tightly together and sealed. Bags and coats were caught between train doors preventing trains from moving, causing unnecessary delays. Daily commuting crowds didn't care less. Once seated inside, passengers read newspapers, books, drank coffee, listened to music on walkman. The trip into the city wasn't always a pleasant ride. There were panhandlers and peddlers trying to sell you anything including batteries, hand held fans, and incense and oils. Sometimes people cursed each other out for something as simple as stepping on someone's toe, people spat on the floor as if they were on the street, or without warning foul smelling vagrants came into the car. Whenever this happened, people literally ran off the train trying to switch cars. When you couldn't switch cars you had to sit and endure the ride together with the foul scent. You were in New York City.

Sometimes sitting in the train on my way to work, I wondered about this place called New York, the place where so many things happened at the same time; most of all people seemed cold and unfriendly. You basically had to mind your own business – it was the silent language of the city – don't stare into people's faces, books or worse, newspapers. As I adjusted to working in the city so did I have to get accustomed to the daily commute, the environment and new customs of life in a big city. I had to find ways to make my daily travel into the city as pleasant as possible.

One day while standing at a huge intersection in midtown I remember seeing hundreds of people waiting to cross the street. Women were nicely dressed, even men were wearing suits. But on their feet they were all wearing white sneakers and socks. I was convinced *these people must really be crazy. How could they be so well dressed wearing sneakers on their feet?* Only months later when my feet pounded on sidewalks, sometimes having to walk blocks and blocks to meet Anthony did I realise why they wore sneakers. It was the practical thing to do given the amount of time people spent walking in the city. I was beginning to gain a fresh respect for Americans. Once more I thought to myself *they were not only practical; they were smart.*

A few years passed. We celebrated our 8th year wedding anniversary with a small party at our home. A few friends came by to share in the celebration with us. We were making progress. Still, inside me burned; I always wanted more; I wanted the chance to attend school. I wanted to learn more American things and history. I wanted to become more educated. With the deep desire to grow, learn and change, I started to make choices that often took me away from home and my family. I attended workshops I found advertised on billboards or newspapers. I signed up for weekend seminars, and conferences, and soon formed my own networking groups outside the home. My new friends and I met over lunch, dinner; we went to the movies. I took dance classes with them, African dance classes, Samba, and modern dance. I tried to attend college but was turned down several times because at the time I didn't have permanent papers. I became despondent. I promised myself to send in a college application every year until I was accepted. I turned to the study of yoga to compensate for my not being able to attend college; it wasn't my first introduction to the Eastern philosophy; I had become familiar with it in Trinidad. From the practice of yoga, I started growing in new and different ways. At the same time I began experiencing much difficulty in trying to communicate this process with my husband.

Chapter 19

Staten Island

"Whatever the soul knows how to seek, it cannot fail to obtain."

Margaret Fuller

I am sitting in a cozy double seat at Mc Donald's. It is about 5:48pm, the day Tuesday. All day long it's been raining. I don't mind the rain; it makes me think. Besides, places are often less crowded. From here the sky is an unlighted rectangle. It peeps through New York Plaza on one side, and One New York Plaza on the other – Corporate America. I am facing Water and Broad Streets; the two make a perfect 'L'. Traffic moves in a deliberate crawl. There are three ambulance vehicles with blinking lights parked on Broad Street. I don't know why. A few people walk by with umbrellas canopying over their heads. On light FM to which the radio is tuned, Celine Deon sings, "My Heart will go on", the theme song from "Titanic". Lovely, I think. Her voice seems even lovelier this afternoon.

There are not many people here this evening. Perhaps it's the rain, I conclude. I am having tea, fries and a grilled chicken sandwich. I won't eat the fries, too much salt! They come with the deal meal. You have to choose for yourself what is healthier. A black couple sits on my left. The gentleman is wearing a navy suit, white shirt with matching navy and gold tie. His voice is mellow; he is well spoken. They are married. I confirm this when I glance at their matching gold rings. The conversation centres on his family, and some problems they are having. "So how do you feel about it?" the wife asks. "I really don't know," he answers, then adds, "I was surprised..." I have no idea what is going on. He continues to talk about his father with whom he seems close, and also his sister. I block them out. It's easy to switch off the talk. From here, in this public space, sipping hot tea, I sit; breathe in deeply, and again, slowly tuning out the day and what's around. I turn the page, take up my pen, and begin to write. Two hours later, alone I gaze through the window with no particular thought in mind, except the commute home to Staten Island.

The first time I visited Staten Island, my mother accompanied me. The year was 1988. She, Miguel and I had travelled to the USA to visit with my sister. My mother took me to visit one of her cousins with whom she had lost touch over the years. She had only seen him whenever he visited the islands. He was a retired school teacher who lived alone. From the moment we met, and he greeted my mother while totally ignoring me, despite the fact she said, "This is my daughter, Sue-Ann, the youngest one," well I didn't like him. He made no attempt to even shake my hand, and I wondered to myself *did he have any manners at all, this retired schoolteacher?* That evening he drove from Staten Island to my Aunt Theresa's home in Brooklyn to pick us up because my mother had promised to spend a few days with him and catch up on old times. We were already packed when he arrived at the door. So without any delay and after those brief introductions we went with him.

My mother sat in the front seat; Miguel and I sat in the back. I was already weary from her cousin's non-stop conversation with her. I already figured out he was lonely. On his visits with my mother in Tobago while on vacation, he had told her she was welcome to his home any time she wanted. She used the opportunity of her trip with us to the USA to visit with him because she had us for company. I was partly awake and partly asleep when I set eyes from a distance of the Verrazano Bridge. It was majestic, built between 1959 and 1964. From the time of its inception I was not as yet born; in 1964 when it opened I was two with no idea about America, let alone living on Staten Island. The bridge separated Staten Island from the other four boroughs. It was named after Giovanni da Verrazano, an Italian explorer and first European navigator who entered the New York harbour. It is the largest suspension bridge in the world. Imagine at the time of its inception it cost just 50 cents to cross the double decked roadway, its longest span being 4,260 feet which carries six lanes on the upper and six lanes on the lower level; today it costs $10.

When I enquired, Sonny Boy, the name I heard my mother call him, said that's where we were heading, right over the bridge. I sat up and took in every sight until we were driving right over the bridge, and I still could not believe my eyes – suspended with steel posts and metal. From the car, we could see ships in the distance, harbour lights, the calm of the ocean. Miguel became excited by the lights. *Where were we going? This Staten Island must be some great place, how lucky my mother and me were to be going in a car to Staten Island.* These were some thoughts flooding my mind, even as we stopped at the tollbooth and Sonny Boy explained he had to pay to cross the bridge. "We are almost there!" he exclaimed. His voice was deep and irritating. Anxiety alone was not all I felt, but could not explain everything. I was also a bit dizzy from the long drive across the bridge, not having driven in a car for about two weeks since leaving Trinidad. I was almost adjusted to subway rides as the norm of public transportation in New York.

My first impressions of driving through Staten Island were that it seemed like Trinidad. I didn't see any huge scary looking apartment buildings, and most of all there was nature, lots of it. Tall trees lined wide streets and healthy looking hedges decorated driveways. I felt at home. In a few minutes after crossing the bridge, we pulled up in his driveway, and I felt an immediate sense of relief it wasn't an apartment. The area we drove around reminded me of the housing development in which Anthony lived, in Trinidad, Diamond Vale. Houses were separated with garages, mailboxes, lawns and lawn decorations, and "Welcome" signs.

Once inside the house, near the doorway we put our stuff down in a corner. I noticed quickly how dusty the place was, even furniture was covered, dining table packed with stuff, things strewn here and there. It didn't seem as if Sonny Boy was expecting company. My idea of having guests was completely out of range with this cousin of my mother's. While he disappeared upstairs for a moment, I silently eyed my mother from the corner where I sat. She had this confused look on her face, but whenever she had that look, it was more a look of embarrassment. We both laughed. *Did he live here alone? Doesn't he clean, or have someone to clean for him?* Quietly my mind wandered off again until my thoughts were interrupted by his voice.

"Pinky, girl, come in the kitchen." He referred to my mother by her home name. "Come on, get up!" my mother waved me off the chair.

We walked through a high archway that separated dining area from the lighted kitchen area. Sonny Boy sat close to my mother. I had Miguel in my arms, he was almost asleep. Sonny boy got up and opened the refrigerator, and then asked whether we were hungry. The refrigerator was packed to capacity with, from where I was standing, what looked like old looking food. He told my mother to go through the refrigerator and see what there was to eat. He also pointed to a bowl full of fresh fruit on the counter top and said "Eat all the fruit, eat whatever you want, drink juice, eat the food!" He repeated this to us after realising we were just listening to him, and not getting anything to eat.

I looked at my mother in disgust, and then at him in a much exaggerated form of disgust *did he think we were hungry? Or came to visit him to be fed? And what does he mean offering us all this old food in the refrigerator, maybe stored there for days?* By that time my mother's eyes searched for mine across the table, she realised she was on her own with her cousin since I slipped into my withdrawal mood. She immediately read my mind, and nicely told Sonny Boy we had just eaten dinner, and we were not at all hungry. It was a lie.

We moved to the living room where Sonny Boy uncovered two chairs, one for me, and a couch where he and my mother sat and chatted. I put my head back on the headrest, stretched Miguel across me; while they talked. We dozed in and out of sleep. During their conversation Sonny Boy asked my mother something about me. When I chimed in to answer he screamed at me saying, "Shut your mouth, I'm not talking to you, can't you see big people talking?" In case he didn't notice, I was a married woman, but with that remark, tears came rushing down my face, and I quickly turned away so my mother would not see them. Then he told my mother we could stay as long as we wanted, and hinted to her she could clean the house, cook, do his laundry, take care of things for him. It then occurred to me Sonny Boy's intention was to make a house keeper out of my mother, maybe even a slave of his cousin, and our stay at his house was repayment for the "good" he was doing for us. When I heard him say this to my mother I had to distract myself because I was so angry I wanted to say some bad words, but what if he put us out on Staten Island, and we had no where to go? *How would we contact my sister?* My thoughts drifted to *Where were we going to sleep? Is he crazy? What if he tried to hurt us in the middle of the night?* I tried hard not to imagine the last thought. Then I heard Sonny Boy saying to my mother he had a mattress in the basement which he would bring up for us. For one thing, I was glad we were not going upstairs with him. At least we would be closer to the front door. I was close to more tears. From what I had already seen I didn't even want to see the mattress, much more to sleep on it. I wanted to return to Brooklyn. The lure of the Verrazano Bridge I had seen earlier and loved had deceived me. I wanted to get out of Staten Island. By the time the mattress was brought from the basement into the living room, there was so much dust flying around, we three had to leave the room while Sonny Boy dusted, and got the mattress ready for us to sleep in the middle of his living room. When he returned and retired for the night it was near midnight. My mother told him she had to call my sister to let her know we had arrived safely, and he told her she could use his phone.

As soon as he trotted upstairs and shut his bedroom door, my mother walked towards me and hugged me, telling me how sorry she was, that she didn't know he was a mean person, and she will get us back to Brooklyn. She tried to explain it was because his wife had passed away, his children lived away from him, and it was because of his loneliness he got this way. She said he was lonely. But I didn't care. I already concluded he was a mean person. I wanted to run far away from this man. My mother searched for her address book and called my sister. On the phone my mother, my sister and I concocted another lie. The first lie was telling Sonny Boy we had eaten when we had not. The second was to make an arrangement with my sister for her to call the next morning and tell Sonny Boy we had to leave because my mother was getting a job. It was too late for my sister to make arrangements to take us to Brooklyn that night since my mother didn't want to create a stir.

The next morning, bright and early, Sonny Boy told my mother her daughter was on the phone, "The big one," he said. Then we heard my mother answer "OK, OK. A real job! Yes, I could do it! You'll pick us up, OK. We'll be ready!" My mother put the phone down. She calmly explained to Sonny boy my sister had a job for her; she had to come right away. Then I watched and listened to my mother explain to Sonny Boy she should take the job because things in Trinidad were hard, and she was sorry to have to leave so soon. I knew my mother had diplomatic skills. In less than half an hour my sister came by with her friend to take us away from my mother's cousin. My sister Susan didn't get out of the car. Miguel and I were already standing on the lawn, waiting for their arrival. I didn't say goodbye to my mother's cousin. But I heard my mother thanking him, and politely telling him she'll call him before leaving the USA.

Once in the car my mother let her guard down with my sister and her friend. She told them how shocked she was both by the way Sonny Boy lived, and also by him thinking he was getting a servant out of her. She said he seemed so nice, always talking about family and what he could do to help them out. But his idea of helping was not the same as ours. I didn't want to hear his name again. That afternoon hearing about our ordeal on our first visit to Staten Island, my sister's employers invited us over for dinner. They were a middle class American family of four with one older daughter, Chloe and one son, Miles. They lived at 166 Benzigger in a two family home I came to know and visit many times. Since my sister had been working for them, and got along quite well, they wanted to meet my mother, son and me.

I was still getting accustomed to having dinners American style; we were so used to everything being homemade, cooked, and well seasoned that sometimes I could barely eat especially in the summer when I witnessed people put slabs of meat and chicken onto the grill without thoroughly washing and seasoning the meats. Many times I left these affairs which my sister dragged us to still as hungry as when we first dropped by or I settled for children's meals mostly of hotdogs, chips and juice. At the Feinberg's because my sister worked for them, she eventually showed them a few things around the kitchen with regard to cooking, and quite often she prepared full meals for them. In no time, they were eating meals prepared West Indian style, and loving it. We had a wonderful dinner with my mother and my sister's boss, Mary talking and talking and liking each other. Our delightful visit with the Feinberg's was the first experience that changed my mind about Staten Island, and some of the people who lived there.

After living in Brooklyn for about six months, Anthony, Miguel and I moved from Brooklyn to Staten Island when we found a small family second floor home for rent on Targee Street. My sister was the one regularly checking the newspaper for apartments. It was a two and half bedroom with kitchen and living room. The moment I saw the apartment I liked it; I would have liked anything that didn't have hundreds of people living in it. We got the apartment, and the three of us moved from St. John's Place to Staten Island, leaving Auntie Jane and Uncle Horace behind, thanking them for their kindness to us, but eager to get on with our own lives. I liked the space in Staten Island; it wasn't cramped, there were not as many apartment buildings on Staten Island as there were in Brooklyn, which meant the place was less crowded. The island was self-sufficient even though cut off from the other four New York City boroughs. The thing that made me want to live there was the closeness of nature. I believed the place was ideal for raising a son.

Staten Island was dominated with the presence of Italian/American, Jews, Irish Catholic, a few Indians from Pakistan and India, and Blacks. There was a Spanish presence, but in the early 1990s not many Mexicans. The influx of Mexicans became more noticeable whenever I saw mostly family homes and private buildings being constructed. Later Mexicans were also used for making home improvements and landscaping. The other thing that became obvious was cheap labour. Early in the morning Mexicans lined corner streets waiting for transportation to job sites. Mexicans were being used since most of them were undocumented and referred to as *illegal aliens.* I never appreciated the term since contrary to Webster's meaning of a person who is not a citizen of the country in which he [she] resides; I on the other hand referred the phrase to something that was not human. Taking an anthropological view, I saw this as another way for exerting dominion over people who were *different* and also *vulnerable.* What seemed more pronounced to me was the fact politicians used these words to control masses of people in much the same way, as is evidenced when studying histories of the native peoples in the USA.

Both Anthony and I worked in Manhattan, this meant having to find day care for Miguel. There was a Spanish woman living with her family across the street who we met and became friends with over time. We later discovered she took care of children. Once we asked her, she willingly took Miguel in, and before we realised he was learning to speak Spanish. We owed much gratitude to this lady named Nancy, who became a loving, nurturing nest for our son. Their family seemed close-knit and we met them eventually coming in and out of their home. Nancy cooked up special Spanish meals for our son, and he ate out of her hands. He especially loved fried plantains and yellow rice. She said he was a good boy and most times didn't give any trouble. Though it was hard I learned to trust Nancy with our son, to let go, the more I trusted the more I realised Miguel benefited from that trust. We all shared a good relationship.

When he turned four we decided to send him to school, Pre-K 4 at Trinity Lutheran. We chose the Lutheran school only because there was an after school programme that ended at 6.30pm. While it was extremely expensive, it gave us enough time to get from the City and pick him up. I will not forget the first day we took Miguel to Trinity Lutheran. The schoolyard was crowded with parents and children. The playground was nicely decorated with coloured swings and slides. Children screamed as sad and guilty parents left their children behind; they had no choice but to leave them in the hands of strange faces, their new caregivers. We put Miguel down, and watched as he ran up towards the entrance, scarcely looking back. The teacher put out her hand; our son ran towards her. Then it seemed she told him to wave to mummy and daddy. The toddler gazed up at us, waved us goodbye, blowing a kiss from his tiny hand. Not a single tear. From that moment I knew we had a different child. At the end of his first day his teacher reported he was *just* fine. We were amazed.

On the weekend we attended mass at the church of the Immaculate Conception, only about two blocks from where we lived. Sunday morning mass was nice; it put you in a good mood for the rest of the day. We returned to a home-made breakfast of scrambled eggs, sizzling bacon, home-style fries; my sister treated Miguel and I to perfectly made round pancakes. My sister usually prepared breakfast for us because by the time we returned from mass she had come home for the weekend, or she might have come in the night before. She was always anxious to see her nephew and spend time with him, taking him to the store, spoiling him. We would have lunch later in the day, and maybe go shopping, to the movies or something like that. Or if we didn't have money we would stay at home, depending on the season.

One of my favourite spots was Clove Lake Park. In the spring or summer we packed a picnic bag, cotton sheet, and while I spent most of the day lying on the grass, reading and writing, Miguel rode his bicycle up and down or played Frisbee with his father, met friends and talked, raced each other, threw pebbles in the lake. I remember soft winds, warm sunshine and eighty degree days. On such afternoons I lay down on freshly cut grass mixed with earthy smell of damp dirt beneath a small bare tree, the same one I've laid under many summers past. On the lake, the sun's reflection was a golden inner pool, inviting me in from the distance. The water was still; there were one or two ducks swimming. Every now and then when I glanced up, the sky was a brilliant blue. Many birds soared. Whenever there were not many people at the lake, those afternoons were pure magic.

When he was five, we took Miguel out from Trinity Lutheran,

and put him in Our Lady of Good Counsel on Victory Boulevard. By that time I had heard too many horrible stories about public school life, to even trust our son to go there without many close friends or family living on the island. He was just a child. Both Anthony and I had a Catholic education all our lives. We knew there would be long-term benefits for our son. But in Trinidad we didn't pay for our education, it was free. Here in the USA, with an after school programme until 6pm it was costly, but a necessary sacrifice we decided had to be made. My sister's employers had both their children attending Our Lady of Good Counsel so when my sister asked her, Mary gladly recommended us, and put our names on the waiting list before the year Miguel turned five. He was accepted. That way we could both work in the New York City without having to worry about who would pick up or take care of him until we got home each day. He would remain at Good Counsel until he graduated, and was ready to attend high school.

The daily commute from Staten Island to the city was long. We had to take one bus from Targee Street, about fifteen minutes to the ferry terminal; the ferry was twenty to thirty minutes; and then the subway from lower Manhattan to Mid town, another twenty minutes to thirty minutes. During rush hour while the ferry schedule was usually consistent, from time to time there were delays caused by broken down boats with mechanical problems, which caused frustration and unhappy commuters. In addition to which people who lived on Staten Island paid double fares. In those days it was financially draining.

We struggled living from paycheck to paycheck with school fees for Miguel, transportation for both of us, and the cost of living increasingly on the rise. But I never wanted to move from Staten Island. It became a home away from home. I was comfortable, happy, and on the weekend whenever I wanted to go into the City, I went. The commute was not a problem or burden for me. I made it less boring by finding things to do. In the beginning, I read newspapers. Soon I found this habit quite upsetting, taking in too much bad news early in the morning. So I wrote checks, slept, or chatted with daily riders. Later, I started writing journals, poetry, stories, and chapters. I noted ferry incidents, watched pigeons, fed pigeons in the terminals, observed commuters, and listened to myself. I planned days at a time, what I was going to cook, made shopping lists, prepared for my day at work, prioritising tasks. I usually got to work feeling refreshed.

I was not like some of my co-workers always complaining about their horrible commute into the office, relating awful train experiences, having a headache or not feeling well. Many people often asked why I continued to live so far away when it was more convenient to get from Brooklyn or Queens into the city. The truth was the ferry ride from Staten Island into the city each day became time for me; it was meditative. It slowed me down. I moved at a different pace from many rushing around in the city. I took things in. Most of all, it helped to put things about my life into perspective; staring at the water each day calmed my spirit. Sitting next to fellow Staten Islanders every morning and evening constantly assured me we were all in this together. Seeing the vast open sky strengthened me. It gave me good travelling and living karma.

Chapter 20

Journeying Forward

"For years I have endeavored to calm an impetuous tide— laboring to make my feelings take an orderly course— it was striving against the stream"

Mary Wollstonecraft

The afternoon is lovely, the sun warm, wind soft. There are not many people at Clove Lake. It's Saturday, the temperature about eighty. I walk to my favourite spot under the open sky, overlooking the lake. I spread the lime green jacket I'm carrying on the grass, and stretch out beneath a small bare tree, the same one I've laid under for many summers past. The sharply scented fresh cut grass mixed with earth fragrances excites me. On the lake, the sun's reflection is a golden inner pool, inviting me from the distance, my inner-self shining before me.

I can scarcely look up because rays of sunlight blind me. The water is still; there are a few herons. Every now and then when I glance up into a brilliant blue sky, one or two airplanes fly by, Newark just over the Goethals. Birds soar. Not far from me a father proudly sits with his newborn infant resting safely on broad shoulders. I think about this safety, and how essential it is in today's world. The mother ventures near the railed edge of the lake. Momentarily she pauses to look at, perhaps, the two most important people in her life; she smiles, then waves. She seems young, fragile, maybe less than five feet tall; her face is small, still glowing from the aftermath of childbirth. I believe it must be her first child. It seems the experience of having her own family delights her.

Only yards away, an eager six year old wearing a pink helmet that is larger than her tiny head, quickly rides by on a purple and pink funky Barbie tricycle. Her mother, a plump forty something year old woman wearing T-shirt, shorts, sneakers and socks, leads the way; the child's father follows just steps behind. This family is from India or Pakistan because their features seem familiar. Of course I think of my own family, married at twenty-four, pregnant at twenty-five and loving it, bearing a son, and thinking *I had just made it. I had just pulled off this thing called life. I was a woman. My husband and I were the perfect twosome. Happiness had to follow.* What I awakened to was a reality of separateness, and thirst for adventure that over many years of marriage became extremely hard to quench.

"In the middle of the journey of our life I found myself astray in a dark wood where the straight road had been lost sight of"

Dante Augileri 1935

I do not know exactly when it happened, except I can say there was a hollow inside of me that needed to be filled, *years of my lonely wanderings were now cashing in on me. Words, sentences I had scribbled in coloured notebooks or pieces of paper were coming alive, wanting to take something from me, to ask more of me, to invade the safe life I was trying to build for my family and myself* I often imagined. This was the result of spending too much time alone. How else could I explain raw urges to sit daydreaming in a park all day long watching birds, people, children, and families, nothing special? This was not a planned path; rather it was an opening that stretched before me in different ways, through many different beautiful people.

My weekends were spent aimlessly wandering New York City's streets. In the beginning I took my son along, he went everywhere I went, but later and as he grew older he complained about wanting to return home, feeling tired, missing his Dad, and when school sports eventually took him away from us on the weekend, I ventured off alone. I visited museums, went to the movies, ate alone, and made some new friends wherever I went. It was on one of my afternoon walks near the Brooklyn Museum after strolling the lovely Botanical gardens, that I became aware of the rhythmic sound of African drums in the distance.

Enthralled with the call of drums, and following the sound I stumbled upon a group of people gathered in a circle on the sidewalk. Inside the circle, there were two people dancing or playing, moving their bodies to the pulsating rhythm of the drum, and also a group of about six others singing and playing instruments. At first it sounded like Spanish, but when I enquired someone told me it was Portuguese. The motion, song and dance that first appeared to be a beautiful fight, mesmerised me. When examined closely it seemed like something more was happening inside the circle. There was an elderly man who made some moves inside the circle, dancing in tune, looking towards the sky, earth, crowd, singing, and leading players on. Despite his age, he was quick and fit on the floor, spinning, making cartwheels, always with eyes focused. Everyone was neatly dressed in white, long pants with t-shirts tucked inside. Flyers were handed out, and then and there I was invited to the Angola School of Capoeira, located on 14th and 6th Avenue.

After visiting the school the following day, participating in a free two hour class, seeing and speaking with a few students including Master Jao Grange who was the man I had seen dancing, I decided I wanted to try this Brazilian martial-art form, which I learnt was used by slaves as a dance in disguise. What the slaves had been doing was preparing for battle with their white slave owners, while appearing to be having fun. All I had known about Brazil was that it was located in South America, had its own history of slavery, culture and lovely women. On several sea voyages my father traveled there and brought me well-made leather sandals, and hand crafted items. I also knew Brazil was home to some of the best soccer players in the world including the renowned Pelé. I often sat with my uncles to watch World Cup soccer, marvelling at their skill, and endurance, admiring fit thighs and handsome men.

When I came to Capoeira, I came to know a concept linked with history – I came to know and understand a world of spirit and connection with what is unseen, but respected. Learning the Art of Capoeira was also about learning how to be human. Like many art forms, it was a discipline that required concentration and practice. Training was intense and rigorous; a series of jumps, kicks, cartwheels all done in sequence, and in response to your partner's moves while dancing the *ginga* taught many things at once including skill, flexibility, agility and awareness. You quickly learnt never to take your eyes off your opponent, and to always be aware of your surroundings. If you practiced hard and learnt with an open mind, were respectful of your partners, didn't engage in useless fighting with your opponent, you also learnt a most valuable tool: peace and love. This however didn't come overnight, you had to *get it*. Perhaps it was a secret understanding. It happened from the inside out; it was the manifestation of the spiritual world becoming alive in you.

At the time of my studying Capoeira, about twice a week, we also played on Sunday from 2pm in a sacred circle called a *Rhoda*. Inside the circle I also learnt many things about the spirit world including reverence, respect and the sacredness of all life. At

Capoeira I came to know another community, Brazilian. Master Jao Grange was also instrumental in steering me ahead; though we spoke different languages, we deeply understood each other. We shared meals, conversations, laughs and teachings. Whenever I did something wrong for instance in my *ginga,* if I continued into an aggressive move, he'd yell and raise his finger "No, Sue-Ann, *Ginga."* Over many years I came to see what this special man was trying to teach me. It was not a fight; it was a deep human connection. Much of my growth process I owe to Master Jao Grange.

We became a close family at Capoeira School, and later I joined a yoga class. It wasn't the first time I studied yoga, but the difference was my teacher, Brazilian dancer Sylvanna was the perfect combination of teacher, dancer and friend. At school we had students from Japan, Africa, USA, the Caribbean, people who nurtured spirit and heart. Most of these people were vegetarians and practiced whatever form of religious worship they saw fit. Sylvanna helped me put many things about my life and body in order. We danced various African dances, Samba, and stick fight late into evenings. We learnt the art of Shiatsu massage and relied on each other for support. Over shared meals, we talked about our dreams and life was good. I had extended myself way out of my community, and I loved my new friends.

My family life started deteriorating because of the choices I made. Especially on the weekend, I spent more and more time away from home. My husband was invited to Capoeira several times, but visited only once, and decided on his own it was not something good. I continued training, learning, and of course growing. My sister grew worried and without understanding mentioned I was going down a wrong path. *How do we decide which path is good or not? Who decides our fate?* I wasn't. When my mother visited me, I had been going to Capoeira School for about two years. I took her to Capoeira where she met Master Jao, my friends and extended family around the drum circle; her eyes were filled with water, and she whispered, "You are a spiritual seeker, I'm so proud of you." My mother knew and understood things I had not imagined. Perhaps my mother did her own spiritual wanderings; her support made my spiritual explorations more worth the journey.

My husband eventually believed if I was spending so much time away from home there might be someone new in my life; there wasn't. I was being quenched spiritually, and it became something no matter how hard I tried to explain, I could not. He listened to some of our friends ramblings about time spent away from home, and what it could mean. But they were wrong. I wanted my family to also share in my spiritual growth. But I didn't try to convince anyone about what I was doing. *How can you explain matters of the soul that really had nothing to do with anyone?* I was focused inwardly; my spirit was calm. I wasn't good at explaining. After all it was my life. I always felt the only thing that belonged to me was my life, and while we chose to share our lives with a person, our life still, and should always belong to us. Perhaps I was naïve to think my husband would sit by. He wasn't at all convinced about my growth process. My husband was set in his ways; he wanted to have the same friends; go to the same social functions, and live the same life we had lived for eight years in the USA. He was comfortable with the familiar.

On the other hand, I was making friends with uncertainty. My husband and I became distant to each other. I could no longer share with him what was important to me because those things had also shifted for me. It wasn't that I no longer cared; my life was taking fresh turns, and while I wanted our marriage I could not take sole responsibility for it not working. We talked less, and whenever we spoke at all it escalated into accusations about what he believed I was involved in. *How could I explain what had shifted inside of me when I didn't even understand it myself? How could I tell him I was happier with my new life? Did I still want my marriage? Would time put things into perspective for me?* Life at home became strained and when Master Jao noticed the difference in my demeanour at class he grew worried. I studied Capoeira for more than five years. It was a form in praise of the ancestors. This was my learning and understanding of the ancient art.

In September 1994, Anthony and I celebrated our eight-year wedding anniversary. We had a few friends over to share this memory with us. But in the months that followed the celebration we grew further apart like two unknown people travelling on different subway lines with little chance of meeting. In December of that year, I took Miguel to a friend's home in New Hampshire. Sarah was a friend I met at Capoeira, and knowing I was having problems at home, she invited me to spend Christmas with her family. Since coming to the USA, it was the first Christmas my family and I spent apart. Miguel and I packed and left home a few days before the holidays. It was a sad choice to make, but somehow I knew I had to make it. We spent Christmas with Sarah and her wonderful family. It was a warm, cozy, American Christmas, one I could never forget.

By the time we got home after Christmas there was a hole so far and wide between Anthony and me it became virtually impossible for us to live together. I had been talking with a Jamaican woman I met at the bus stop each morning as she waited for the bus. I played with her daughter, Lisa in the stroller; her son, Jaime also attended Our Lady of Good Counsel. After talking with her over months at the bus stop, Novia told me if I ever needed a place to stay, she would help me. But the idea of leaving my home seemed near impossible. I didn't have the courage, and how would I tell Anthony I was leaving? But I was unhappy; days dragged on, and I spent nights wondering where we went wrong. How could this happen?

Almost one year later in 1995, three important things happened that impacted our family life: together with my son I moved in to Novia's living room space which she converted into a bedroom for us; for the first time I was accepted into the City University of New York to pursue a Bachelor's Degree; and I walked out on an eight year old marriage.

Chapter 21

Education

"I am careful not to confuse excellence with perfection. Excellence, I can reach for; perfection is God's business."

Michael J Fox

Today Gladys and I met for lunch. She and I became friends after 1995. We took a Poetry Workshop in New York City. The class was conducted in the conference room of the New York Public Library on 5th Avenue. Our teacher, Nicole Liberman didn't seem enthused to greet her new class. I remember thinking *Gosh, she looks so mean,* and to make myself feel better even thought *maybe she just had a bad day!* About twenty of us, still strangers to each other, sat on comfortable puffy chairs around a long wooden table.

As an introduction to the class we were told to bring one original poem together with twenty copies. We did. Nicole had little trouble laying down ground rules. The workshop was scheduled to run from September until the spring; more than three consecutive absents were grounds for dismissal. It was the FREE admission that lured us into the class. We were told, when our turn came around we would each read our poem aloud. The floor was opened for discussion and critique during which time the poet could not speak, but was allowed to take notes on ideas for suggestions and improvements. After critiquing, the poet was given time to respond to comments made, and offer explanations about lines, words, beats or titles. The final decision for changes to the poem was left solely in the hands of the poet.

I easily recall the moment when Gladys read her poem for the first time, how harsh criticisms seemed, and so much the same when I also read. Somehow though many did not, we both had enough guts to return to class the following Tuesday. I could still hear Nicole's sharp words warning us if we wanted to write, we had to be prepared for criticism. After months of trying our hands at the craft and re-trying, pining and learning. Three years passed. Both Gladys and I survived the class long enough to hear Nicole say with soft emotion, and even a gentle smile "Lovely poem Gladys," and "You're becoming an interesting poet Sue-Ann." We responded with proud "Thank yous." Well on those nights we bubbled from the library, hugged each other and comforted our egos. Eventually we parted. Neither Gladys nor I could take those classes any longer. We would miss them – we would miss each other. We continued on our separate journeys, meeting in the city occasionally for tea to share new discoveries and frustrations.

When we met, Gladys told me in February she'd turned seventy-five. "How happy you must be," I said enclosing my arms around her tiny frail neck. As she started to mumble "Well I'm not young anymore…" I interrupted "I hope you live to be…my grandmother is about eighty. The women in our family have a history of outliving the men." Gladys replied "Oh Sue-Ann you're so sweet thanks." Lunch was wonderful – time, well spent.

The same afternoon I met with one of my professors at the Graduate Center on 5th Avenue at 34th Street, just a walk from the office. Two semesters ago, I had two B's on my class papers, so I asked him whether there was anything I could do to improve the grades. He told me he could give me an incomplete, and I could work with him on another subject of interest. Since I worked in the City, and because he also had an office at the Graduate Center, we agreed it would be a convenient meeting place. He was an interesting professor (Anthropology); he wrote on *The Lumbee Indians*, and quite understandably had an extremely hectic schedule. I didn't realise how much extra time was involved in independent work, but I have been patient. Lately I had been learning more about virtue. I didn't miss any of my appointments with Professor Sider; he often lent me tapes from which I extracted a world of information. I usually sat in his office reading something new (on Native American Indian history) while he graded my written papers.

We discussed the paper I handed in. He let me know how I could have improved on the work, how I could have connected paragraphs and linked them to the main theme. I thought carefully about what he said. The word *flow* came to mind. The paper was based on Indian peasants living in Mexico. They responded to the Zapaista calling because of their ongoing struggle for justice. Professor Sider was pleased with the paper and in particular with the conclusion. Since I had re-written it several times over the last few months, I was relieved. I breathed hard. He graded the paper with an A-. I exhaled. Now I wondered *why did professors have to put that minus sign after an A?* We discussed the second paper. I jotted down relevant points on which I had to focus. The paper dealt with the *Cheyenne.* The *Cheyenne* people lived on the Plains, central Algonkian provenience on the Canadian side of the Great Lakes. The word *Cheyenne* came from *Sioux* and according to Webster's means those who speak an unintelligible language. That was how Native American Indians were viewed. I mentioned to him how important it was to finish the paper because unknown to both of us the "Incomplete" was calculated as a "Fail" on my transcript. This lowered my GPA. It was the first time my GPA had been affected. Professor Sider understood.

Since Anthropology, the study of humans in their environment fascinated me from the start, I told Professor Sider what I had been meaning to for a long time but was still a bit timid. I mentioned how intrigued I was by his wealth of knowledge and genuine interest in the native people of the Americas. The chance for me to study native peoples, culture, environment, gender and more spurred my questioning of things. I informed him when my assigned work was completed I would like him to suggest a new assignment. He was happy to hear this and agreed. Off the top of his head he mentioned a few topics that might interest me: role of women as "constructed" as a means to encourage, promote and sustain universal subordination; fear for extending full equality between the sexes; then we discussed the plight of Irish Catholic women who were imprisoned in Northern Ireland in their struggle for independence. In order to transcend traditional gender boundaries, those women prisoners smeared prison walls with their faeces and menstrual blood, as a symbol of being "dirty" to prevent themselves from being raped; they protected themselves by using their bodies. Such subjects engaged my thought processes and impacted my world view.

We talked for a while about the Silence of Native American Indian People. We spoke about their commitment to maintain silence about their past, their silence that was so much a part of their way of living. Professor Sider shared with me the fact, as a Jew, his parents and grandparents never discussed their past. In fact if they had to in his presence, they did so in their native tongue. He admitted it was a shame. I asked him whether those silences were related in some way to the silences many women across the globe were forced to endure. I shared with him as a young child I also remembered I was not born Catholic. My grandmother said her prayers in a certain part of the house. We were Hindu, my grandfather was Muslim, and my ancestors came from Northern India to work as indentured labourers in the cane fields in Trinidad and Tobago. I told him I used to stand beside my grandmother, holding on to her dress, quietly watching. I would often mumble jumbled prayers after her, some she recited in Hindi.

Later when there was new talk of the church and the word Catholic mentioned the shrine was removed from our home. I told him how I used to stand at the empty space wanting to pray while my grandmother shouted at me saying "Little girl, what yuh lookin' for? There is nothin' there!" My professor admitted some of the questions we explored were not easily solved. I pondered quietly in his presence. "Indeed," I said. "Over a lifetime, perhaps."

The more I immersed myself in my studies, the more I changed, and made different choices. Some path had opened before me, and I wanted to give myself the chance for exploration. Not that I had any idea of where I intended to land, but more, I wanted to check things out for myself. Living in the USA had become something with meaning and purpose. I had intentions— dreams. Just like thousands who before me left their homeland in search of something "better" as part of the American dream, I wanted to use the opportunities before me.

It was the exchange of culture and difference that became important to me. If I could just show America more about the place from which I came, the tiny twin islands in the Caribbean. In return I would learn as much as was possible for me, and there would be genuine progress. At school I endeavoured to always give it my best shot. I never failed a class, did not settle for less than I was capable of accomplishing, and pushed myself over years of undergraduate studies. Professors were amazed; they admired my attentiveness and willingness to learn. I reciprocated by participation and making honest comments. Progress for me was slow; I was not travelling in the fast lane; in fact sometimes I didn't even believe I was making strides. Over time, understanding came... just like in the story of *The Velveteen Rabbit* by Margery Williams, "...bit by bit until all your hair has been loved off." I started to unravel, learn and grow in many different ways.

Because I attended school on a part-time schedule while also working a forty-hour week, by the time I earned my Bachelor's Degree, seven years had passed. Those years were tough;

schedules demanded much of me and finances dwindled. But through this process I became even more self disciplined. It became noticeable. Some people remarked I believed I was perfect. For me it wasn't about perfection; the only person I compared myself with was me. I was trying to be the best I could be. While some believed I had "an attitude;" it was just I had to make different choices. School wasn't a drag; papers were not boring or hard, but rather challenging and worth discussions that followed. I left work at 4.30pm, caught an express bus to Staten Island, slept on the bus, and then attended a double class from 6.30pm until 10.15pm three nights a week. I arrived home around 11.10pm having to prepare for the next day, packing books and noting assignments while trying to also get some rest before the routine repeated itself the next day. This continued for seven years. I used my sick days for studying and resting; vacation days were used for exam studying or group study. Time was never wasted. I had no social life except what was created at school. There was little time for my family and my husband had no choice but to pick up the slack where taking care of our son was concerned. It didn't matter when I graduated so long as I was enjoying my studies; I didn't place any time lines on myself. I was growing from the inside out. This was my time and it had little to do with others, it was my choice. I owed it to myself.

Whenever study abroad opportunities were posted, I took advantage of the first chance to study at the University of Hawaii at Hilo. It was worth every penny we paid for hiking over craters, volcanic rock, and visiting Hawaii Volcanoes National Park. After a full breakfast during which time we filled up with carbohydrates, we left campus by 8am with a full schedule. On campus, breakfast was buffet style. My favourite dish was some kind of Hawaiian sticky rice with a vegetable omelette, some fresh fruit, juice, tea and anything nourishing we felt like filling up on. We were forewarned of long morning hikes that lasted many hours.

We hiked over Mauna Loa and Mauna Kea summits; we

visited the site of Kilauea volcano, became mesmerised hiking over huge craters, observing from a distance steaming vents and molten lava. We marvelled at waterfalls, rainforests, flora and fauna that have formed because of the changing ecosystems. Professor O'Han from the College of Staten Island, our Geology teacher made such one in a life time trip interestingly possible; his knowledge and passion in showing students first hand how the five islands were formed was admirable. We were well prepared for hikes. We travelled with weather resistant hiking boots, sneakers and socks; rain gear; umbrellas; sunscreen and sunglasses, light cotton to layer, and of course cameras. We had backpacks and quickly realized after our first hike what to take with us for each road trip. Exhausted we returned to campus every afternoon, rested a few hours only to later engage in classroom sessions for discussions, notes and itinerary for the following day.

Some native Hawaiians were not welcoming to American students; we sometimes encountered hostility on the streets. On one such occasion, a small woman only about five feet tall who you would least expect walked up to our professor, looked him in the eye, then spat right in front of him. Professor O'Han was tall, way over six feet; the woman looked up to him. We were appalled. He was a good man, working hard, doing good things with his knowledge and wisdom. She didn't care. Our professor did not create a scene. He simply walked away. Our days in Hawaii were transforming. The ocean was exactly what was reported in travel brochures and magazines; heavenly. We hiked over hills, and swam in the ocean. We visited a black sand beach, and also a green sand beach. The view from hiking above was pure magic.

Since I also believe in the spirit world, I must share the Legend of Pele, the goddess of fire who was believed to have lived in the Halema'uma'u crater of Kilauea. Legend has it that the goddess Pele is beautiful; she can be calm and can also erupt. Her nature is one of volatility. Her home is in the pit of one of the most active volcanoes on Earth. But it is also believed she controls all volcanic activity. I remembered praying to her for our safe passing whenever we traversed the island, and especially hiked over craters for miles.

With a sweet taste left in my mouth from the Geology trip to Hawaii, several months later I found myself reading notice boards at school, looking for another study abroad programme. The trip to Shanghai, China was posted and for the second time an opportunity to study abroad presented itself. At the University of Shanghai and for six credits the courses offered were Mandarin and Business. Almost immediately I wrote letters seeking scholarship funds to help offset travelling, room and board, and course costs. Not many students applied; I wondered why. I won a scholarship to attend. Together with nine students from the City University of New York, which meant they attended universities within the five boroughs, our group convened for orientation at the College of Staten Island. Program Coordinator Russell Davis met and discussed with us flight arrangements, insurance, how much money we needed, what to expect once we landed in China, what was expected of us, what necessary items to pack and so on. The group met each other. Only a few months later, we left New York just after Christmas on December 26 through Newark, headed for Los Angeles, where we connected with Eastern China Airlines for a flight to Shanghai China. Flying to China was incredible. The trip from Los Angeles to China, while long and tiring, was memorable. We travelled over the Alaska Glaciers, witnessed the most magnificent sunset beyond the horizon near Hawaii. At one point when you gazed through the airplane towards the glorious horizon, and you stared in awe at the wonder of being so close to the sky you actually felt you could simply walk off the airplane. You marvelled at the pilots who took you safely across mountains and gigantic oceans. You were in awe. That was how I started making my private dreams come true – with each step. I was no longer living in a dream like state, but was instead alive and walking through each lived experience.

The time we spent in China was enriching. While we studied we also visited many interesting sites such as The Temple of 500 Buddha; the Bund; and the Pearl Telecommunication Station. The Bund was a fantastic site of the waterfront in the fast changing city with cool places for strolling, meditating, kiosks for shopping and also exploring the great buzz of Shanghai. At the Silk Factory, apart from touring the place, we were treated to a fashion show and had the opportunity of purchasing fine Chinese silk. One day trip we travelled to the villages of Suzhou and Hangzou. In Suzhou we toured luscious gardens nestled between water and rock. It was an artist's paradise in rich earth tones celebrating great Mother Earth with reflections of sea and sky. This visit quieted my spirit and fed my creativity. Walking alone in a bonsai garden I met an elderly Chinese woman with whom I sat and without conversation we stared deeply into each other's eyes, just acknowledging our humanity and the fact we were both at the same time in the presence of such wondrous beauty. At Hangzou we toured the Six Harmonies Pagodas, took hundreds of photographs taking in landscapes and sceneries and quiet lakes we had only dreamt of before. The history of Hangzou spans some two thousand years; many architectural structures were built in the Song Dynasty.

In the city of Shanghai we travelled by train experiencing the maddening rush and dash for the train among hundreds. It was frightening because all you felt was being pushed with the crowd onto the train. When shopping, we eventually acquired the skill of good bargaining. Although in the beginning many of us got caught in the web of trickery – some ended up being robbed rather than obtaining a good bargain. We partied and travelled alone, though mostly in pairs, navigating our return to the campus by practicing the newly acquired skill of speaking Mandarin. Some of us even had our hair done at Espirit in China; it was a huge out-of-this-world salon, giving us freebees of t-shirts, bags, and hair products for attending their salon. Noticeable in the city of Shanghai was the symbol of American capitalisation: McDonald's, KFC, Banana Republic and the newly established Starbucks. We were pleasantly surprised. Such chains were appreciated because after weeks on a Chinese menu, some of us desperately devoured a burger and some fries.

When offered a home stay weekend experience many American students did not wish to leave campus to spend time in the home of a native Chinese student. I on the other hand jumped at the chance to experience the culture outside of school. Once we got there, her father was already preparing us dinner. It was about an eight course meal. We quickly settled into her room and got ready for dinner. Their home was a newly built luxurious concrete space with spacious rooms, high ceilings and humble décor. It was an awakening for me. Dinner was wonderful; we had shrimp, crab, and lobster, several kinds of rice dishes, vegetables I recognised and some I did not, and cups and cups of tea. After dinner we shared Chinese sweets, and as is customary, we exchanged gifts. Since we had been previously advised, we brought gifts from the USA such as things not made in China: US chocolates, stamps and locally made trinkets. This was a particularly hard exercise for us having to shop in the USA for authentic "Made in the USA" items. We soon discovered how much of USA imports depended on China, a very important business lesson.

The following morning, I was lucky to have had the rare chance to attend a traditional Chinese wedding, since my hostess's cousin was about to be married; the family seemed well off. Attending a traditional Chinese wedding in China gave me yet another glimpse into a culture that has tremendous tradition and deep significance embedded in history. From spending the entire morning at the bride's home in Pedong District, observing and eating all morning, to later in the afternoon travelling miles through scenic country terrain to the groom's home in Zabei District where a lavish ceremony was held, I was filled with wonder and excitement. The groom was a handsome Chinese man; his home was newly built for his bride; it was splendid. We sat to a lavish meal, several courses including snake soup and other sea creatures I was unfamiliar with to even try were served. The moment I believed the wedding was over I was in for yet another surprise. Late that evening we drove for about one hour to downtown Shanghai where a new ceremony took place at the New Asia Hotel, followed by more cocktails, and a full twelve course dinner party. By that time I had gone to the bathroom several times, I didn't think I could survive the evening's festivities. Sitting at the wedding table with bride, groom, hostess, close family and friends, I felt honoured in the moment. I spent the time at the table mostly smiling with guests, taking notes, holding and shaking hands, getting up to meet more family, and being careful not to eat much more food. Returning to campus on Monday morning, I came away from the home stay with another perspective of accepting difference and finding balance.

At graduation, the Dean of the University in China, Zhang Xijiu mentioned we were a lucky bunch since we saw two years in China. We didn't understand. What she meant was we ended 2001, and started 2002 in one trip. She mentioned sometimes such opportunities came only once in a lifetime. I was thankful to be in the presence of a woman of deep wisdom and understanding. She and I later had a one-on-one conversation about China, education and the chance we had to be present at their University. On behalf of all the students present I thanked her and the University for the hospitality and warmth extended during our stay; I thanked the Business Professor Wei Jinluan, and especially our Mandarin Professor, Xue Lao for being patient with us during class time when some students were late or didn't complete an assignment. Unlike the experience in American classrooms, information coming in to the classroom in China was seriously filtered. There were hardly candid discussions about hard issues, most especially, politics.

Since I was one of the older students on the trip I explained some of the students were quite young to distill some of the deeper perspectives of the trip, but I hoped in time they all would. I stressed we were happy to have seen China in two years. The experience in China broadened my panoramic view of the world and its people tremendously, especially since Chinese people also emigrated to Trinidad and Tobago. Having the chance to glimpse the other side of the world, live in the same world as twelve million people do in the City of Shanghai, eat similar food, and also study helped me interpret the world at new levels.

Continuing my studies, I had a weakness for books. I traded haircuts and shopping events for purchasing books. Books spilled over shelves unto the floor of my living room, packed into boxes and bins. Books had information from fact, fiction, drama, philosophy, politics, world news, events, drama, beauty, health, and fitness, anything I wanted to learn about. Life was interesting; learning made me happy. This was before Google and the wealth of information accessible on the internet with the click of a mouse. I was changing as I unveiled, making myself flexible to opportunities before me. The universe had opened up before me in remarkable ways, and I was responding. I often noticed whenever I leapt forward or toward some new pursuit, the universe magnified for me in unimaginable ways, making obstacles only efforts away from real accomplishments. Learning took new colours and shades of understanding as I tried to distill my thoughts and experiences via the written and spoken word. I was shaping my own worldview not so much by the politics around me, but from my gut, from my centre. I was becoming wholly engaged with life's challenges. Education was alive within me. Most of all, I was comfortable with me.

At our graduation in the summer 2002, keynote speaker and then Mayor of New York City, Mr. David Dinkins spoke about the urgency of obtaining a Liberal Arts form of education. He mentioned how important it was to widen our scope and perspectives. That way he assured us we could become more balanced individuals because we would be trained to be impartial in our thinking. In this way rather than taking a bird's eye view to situations we could outwardly extend our grasp on life. His words confirmed what I already believed. Attending Corpus Christi College in Trinidad had broadened this liberal perspective and given me an advance start on life and learning. Putting into practice all I had learnt: self discipline, attentiveness, my general serious approach to work and study, leadership skills and training gave me an edge to maturity that only few understood.

Of course had I remained in the islands of Trinidad and Tobago I might not have gotten the chance to enhance my experience and learning. The chance to travel to Hawaii and China, to visit different states in the vast USA, to profoundly immerse myself in my studies, and also in culturally exchanging ideas made me more grounded. Several American writers including Ted Conover, Edward Beck, Porter Shreve, Anita Shreve, Derek Walcott and Elizabeth Nunez are only a few who I met and or studied one-on-one with at Penn State University, Sarah Lawrence College, and Marymount College. I travelled out of New York City to attend conferences and seminars at Key West and Stony Brook. I met poets and writers such as Robert Bly and Natalie Goldberg, author of *Wild Child* and *Old Friend from Far Away: The Practice of Writing Memoir*. Their advice and writing helped me move forward. This intermingling of knowledge has been my greatest reward and comfort. It gives me deep satisfaction knowing I have given the best of myself to the USA, and in return I have received nothing but the best. It is the karmic cycle of life. It is my karma. I take full responsibility for my responses in how the cycle of life reveals itself through people and places in my life. I continually feed the drive to write. I nurture its nuisances and have learned to wait, patiently.

Chapter 22
Following Dreams

"Two roads diverged in a wood, and I took the one less traveled by,
and that has made all the difference."

Robert Frost

In the book, "Writing and Cleaning our Minds: Instructions to the cook: A Zen Master's Lessons in Living a Life That Matters," co-authors Bernard Glassman and Rick Fields advise in the present we have everything we need, "in order to see the ingredients we already have in our lives, we need to clear a space." In other words, before cooking a meal, we must clean our kitchens, even though it may already be clean. Clutter creates confusion and can often block clarity. When we take time to clean, we change, our surroundings change, and so do those who come into our spaces. We begin to see new ingredients already present, some that need to be replenished, and more to be discarded.

The process of writing is also a kind of cleaning. Whenever we write, we come closest to ourselves. We are mirrored in every word we put down on the page. We are constantly changing, learning and growing. It is necessary to weed out the dull and lifeless, the not so good. We are constantly filled with ideas, beliefs and assumptions that need repotting. But more importantly is the fact we must replant in rich soil whatever it is that moves us. As writers, we can begin this process by being open to new things, some of which might be different from what we're accustomed to, even strange. We must be prepared to step away from what we think we know, and learn something fresh. The choice to write is the chance to say "yes" to life. While this process may seem difficult, it improves with practice, and becomes a responsibility over time. The more I write, the more attuned I seem to become with myself, and the more I discover many questions to ask. If I choose to listen, I will hear. If I talk too much, I will drown the music.

When I began writing, I began allowing the musing of my soul to be born on paper, I began moving, dancing, loving – sharing dreams, and creating my own visions of things no longer imagined. When I began to allow myself free reign, I became a radical thinker, saying "yes" to my soul, and "no" to what was clearly wrong in the world around me. Night suddenly shone before me in varying hues – I started to see between cracks inside walls I had built around myself, not daring anyone to come in. When I embraced my vulnerability and stood there fully present and naked, I listened to the rain; heard drops softly fall.

When I began to allow the fruits of my labour to blossom and bear fruit, I started to unfold – one word, sentence, each thought progressing from another, perhaps inventing stories about a life lived somewhere before now, or not. Sometimes such thoughts started at the same place, a process. It felt like a growing expansion inside me, a gentle ripple flowing into the swelling ocean, towards the belly of beyond – some deeper existence of where I traveled before. Dreams. Who I was becoming, still unnamed.

When I began writing empty visions of my life were replaced with fresh awakenings, pretending to be alive was no longer an option. The path before me did not always promise certainty, but hope in possibilities spurred me towards the next best experience. The outcome didn't have to be perfect; consequences of honest choice created my reality.

When I began writing I saw my own reflection; tears, unimaginable pain; lies, intensity, my unwillingness to let go. When I began writing I began living at extremes, dreaming crazy things, even watching them unravel – grasping in my hands knowledge I hardly imagined possible. When I began writing I started to live inside each day, seeing myself only as one special lantern among many. When I began writing I started to feel the wind on my naked skin.

At home on Staten Island, I spent most of the day moving awkwardly from table to home computer to the edge of my bed near the ironing board upon which my lap top sits. Peaches, my Terrier-Pekinese is snugly curled inside her basket only seven footsteps away from me; her tiny black head hangs over the edge of a wicker basket. She has grown grey at the chin and belly. Every time I shuffle back and forth her beady black eyes follow me across the room. Lazily she crawls from her basket, shadows me into the living room where I retrieve some books, and return into the bedroom again. I make this circuit many times during the day until Peaches gets weary. She demands more attention by getting into a tail wagging frenzy, barking incessantly until I take her outdoors for a walk. I oblige. Once outside I walk wherever she wants, chasing blackbirds across the driveway, sniffing out freshly cut grass, searching out her favorite spot, barking at dogs three times her size, being petted by passersby. She loves it whenever strangers stop to ask questions about her; she dances about their feet, hopping upon their legs, seeking the spotlight. They never believe she is seventeen; we got her when Miguel was three. The wind outside is cool, the sky bright and baby blue.

Inside again, and while trying to write the last three chapters of this memoir in one sitting words elude me; organisation got the better of me. Whenever I got stuck, I did laundry and cooked, grabbing stacks of mail in between brief walks to the washing machine, trying to pull out bills, separating what was important from what could wait a few weeks. Finishing the story is important not only because I have lived it, but also because it shapes my core. Having come from islands in the Caribbean where people are often believed to be "small minded people," I always believed one day this small minded person will make big connections. I don't think my presence in the USA is a coincidence. I never have. In fact, I believe it was the way set out before me. I saw it then, before moving here. And I see it now. Still, an open field of possibilities.

The more I probed myself for answers about life and my writing, the more I was beginning to understand and realise the work will be ready whenever it is finished. This process will take as long as it has to. It's like when I first started college. I didn't go because I wanted a better job or to earn more income, though perhaps I might. I went to school because from where I had been standing, college was the only place where I needed to be at that particular time. I remember walking along Mid Manhattan one night. Bright stars lighted the sky, and gazing up I saw scribbled across the vast sky "You are going to college."

A couple of friends wanted to go to the movies this evening; I did not. They concluded I didn't take enough breaks; I didn't agree. I told them it was better for me if I remained at home, and continued writing. Disappointed, they gave up. I believe this is how we chart new territories for ourselves, focusing on what we deem important, always moving forward. We create our own histories. This to me is the language of freedom – my excuse for writing, weaving important narratives that affect our daily lives. Most days I enjoy waking up alone. Other times, not. For now I have to matter to me. It is the thing that makes me dance an exciting, and sometimes an excruciating, dance of life. Maybe later, I will matter to most.

On my way home from work, sometimes I went to the upper

deck of the ferry so I would not be disturbed. It was often on such evenings someone approached me "Miss, do you have a pen?" or "Is this your newspaper?" Often, I nodded, and then deliberately gazed through the window across the calming water towards the lighted city. Each night there seemed to be more glimmering lights, shapes and beauty. There was at times live entertainment on the upper deck, which because I'm well acquainted with most acts, I avoided. The weather was warming up, and the ferry ride home was much more crowded. There was a problem with one of the larger boats, *The Marchi* (named after the longest serving US senator; he was a democrat), so they were operating on a three boat schedule. I had the opportunity of meeting Senator John J Marchi one evening at the College of Staten Island as part of our Public Administration class; he was a small man with great ambition and tenacity having worked in the US Senate most of his adult life. I was struck by his simplicity and deep commitment to service.

On the boat, some people talked; those alone read a book, newspaper, wrote checks, snacked or napped. There are Staten Islanders who sat on the same seat everyday and have done so over many years. Younger kids spread themselves across coloured seats. I don't know why some young men wore oversized pants, falling off their asses to expose some labelled underwear that read CALVIN KLEIN or TOMMY HILFIGER, their crotch hanging down to their knees. In many ways we were influenced by the fashion industry; I've already warned my son never to ask me to buy him those type of pants. He won't. In my own case, I wore colours and styles that complemented my personality. I remembered when I first came to the USA; everyone wore black for everything, every day. I remembered thinking to myself *who's dead?* I never assimilated into the wear only black culture, could not. I didn't care what was fashionable or not; I loved colour. I was not a follower.

On the boat, kids told each other about school, sports, family, and about the people with whom they were involved. I watched them tease each other, make jokes, discuss events, and listen to music. I didn't remember thinking this was all there was to life. I was too serious. I believed somewhere out there was more – there were secrets in life which I had to discover. I had always tried to query these things in the friendships I cultivated with people much older than I was – aunts, cousins, friends, and teachers. They, I believed, knew the secrets. I was fascinated about growing older. I wanted to know anything, everything.

At 7:45am some women on the ferry talked about losing weight, diet, and lifestyles. They were loud, raucous, hungry for attention and flattery. They had become obsessed with skinny images of who they should look like and who they should imitate. They mentioned things like Slim Fast, Jenny Craig, diet pills, creams, and purging with the use of laxatives. They talked about this man and that relationship, where they thought he's been, who he was seeing, whether or not he was married, and with whom he was sleeping. Their constant chatter often got heated with loud outbursts of laughter or even in disagreement about who was right or wrong, who felt discriminated against at work, police brutality in the news and always the issue of race came up.

Every day, I listened to some of the same conversations thinking, *No wonder why the world was in the state it was in today. People are much too self-absorbed to think about another person or what's going on. Too much time was wasted in useless talk that did nothing to elevate the positions of women or our circumstances. Instead we left it up to the politicians.* There seemed to be an urgent need for noise and confusion. I remembered watching in disbelief The Jerry Springer Show. I could not believe it was entertainment; at one point it was considered the number one talk show in the USA. People fought on air; chairs were thrown at men by women who were frustrated with their domestic relationships. Young women accused their mothers of stealing their boyfriends; children verbally abused their parents, and a live audience laughed! I think such distractions are deliberately set up to entrap us while consuming our attention. In this way, our focus on more important issues affecting our standard of living for example, education, the rising cost of living, issues affecting the environment and our health, just to name a few, became second nature. Our ability to see beyond the politics inside the politics becomes a blur. As a society we become numb, reacting to things of little significance as the world moves ahead spreading capitalism, wealth and expansion into the twenty-first century, while we, particularly women, were once more left on the edges of society.

Walking along Broadway this evening the air was light and fresh. The street partially deserted with one or two people hurrying past me. When I crossed Rector Street, the setting sun was a huge floating ball that peeped out of the sky between the jagged edges of two corporate buildings. From the distance it was dark orange mixed with hues of red that sent soft ripples down the length of my spine. The sky was white, darkening. No stars.

Further down, some teenage boys, one Asian, the others two black and three white, skateboarded on the sidewalk, practicing various spins, turns, and dangerous jumps. I watched how with knees bent slightly, whenever they leapt from narrow decorated boards, they were suspended a few inches into the air, somewhat clumsily, and then landed back unto the board giggling. They took turns and gave each other thumbs up.

A few hundred yards down, I sat alone on the empty steps of the National Museum of the American Indians at Bowling Green. There I saw how skyscrapers in the area seemed only an arm's length from the sky. It looked like if I had a ladder with about forty rungs, I might climb to the top, reach out and touch the vastness of something I just accept. In the park opposite the museum, a young woman walked two black poodles; express buses to Staten Island sped by, filled. A number of people made their way underground. I sat quietly on the steps and contemplated writing the conclusion to a story that was not yet finished. I recalled many months, years of hard work, paying attention, working on edit suggestions, attending workshops, writer's conferences, and how more work has brought me to this place – the place where I seemed to have understood just a little more. Words such as process, voice, style, language, layers, and plot made more sense to me than when I first started writing. I remembered the seed planted thirteen years ago in class, the urge to write – the urgent necessity. Then I wondered *in terms of writing and me, what's next?* I like to think as a writer I can use my knowledge to help those who did not have such chances for learning. I believed knowledge I have acquired through living in a first world country was intended for this purpose – to share in community – that somehow I was handpicked for this journey.

After living in the USA since 1989, while working in a Trinidad and Tobago environment I can say that while much has changed, some things have remained the same. I still have a strong Trinidadian accent and while I speak English have not adopted an American accent. I understand when Americans speak and Americans often understand what I say. In fact, they've come to appreciate the island accent as part of who I choose to be, most times. But working in a familiar environment you're expected to be a certain way, anything outside of that box is subject for suspicion. Especially as an Indian woman, I did not fit into the box. In other words, the more I assimilated into American culture, immersing myself in subjects other than what was expected, the more people around me became suspicious. In fact it became so obvious at one point rather than try to understand me; it became easier for some people to judge me.

For the most part, I have not fitted the expected role into which I had to conform; I am not simply an Indian woman; I am an educated Indian woman who thinks for herself, strives for independence, and motivates those around her to do the same. I have defied the norm. I am a solution. Education must be active. If I cannot practically apply learning to help improve the lives of those around me, most especially women, then what good is education? As far as I knew myself, I was always chasing some dream, reaching for something I believed I wanted. Committed and open to endless possibilities, I wanted to write, not simply to write without attachment, but also to use writing as a tool to enter the lives of women. This is my language. I wanted to delve into women's histories, disappointments, travails, and their ordinary lives. Writing allows me freedom to shape the narratives.

I was always a quiet person on the inside; you had to do work in order to get to know me; I chose my friends carefully. My stepfather once told me to have few of the best, that way if needed you can count them on your ten fingers and toes. But remember in times of crises, you'll know for sure who can be counted upon to be there for you. It was wise advice. The friends I have today are the same ones I've made decades ago; they have remained constant in my life and through their love, support and understanding have given me much to live for. They challenge my beliefs and accept my passions. The new friends I've made seem fleeting, but over many years from time to time, we still managed to keep in touch. While friends often remind us who we are; real friends are our reflection.

Today, I speak a new language of my own that is continually evolving. It is strong, and wants to find meaning in what is deemed meaningless. The language is the story about a little girl, now a woman, trying to find her way as she journeys through the vast universe. She is always starting something over, *never* perfect. She knows this. Her life is a series of beginnings and failures, of falling down and getting up. It is about getting up. It is about experience, success and shortcomings, heartbreaks, and finding courage to keep forging forward. It is about words and emptiness; power and lack of control. This language moves beyond itself; it strives to be soft and strong balancing what is good, tearing off what is not so good. The language is a constant shedding of myself, of starting over, beginning in a new place or not. It speaks of freedom. It is rooted in identity, higher education, and my insatiable thirst for knowledge. It is my inward search.

One of my best friends settled in Maryland; we were not in the same class at Corpus Christi College, she was my sister's friend, but later she and I became closer through summer hang outs, movies, and weekend trips. When she first came to the USA, she worked for an American family, doctor and lawyer combination with three children. At the time, the children were young boys, the last girl being just one year old. In the beginning what they saw was a young, black, island woman who became their babysitter.

Over time, I marvelled at the strong love and bond this family made with my friend, Felicia. She remained employed with the family for many years, seeing the children through Bah Mitzvas, high school, and she was still employed when the couple later divorced. She comforted the children, cried with them, and they grew with her. She was still working with the family when the eldest child, Jeffrey went off to college.

When her employer sponsored her for permanent resident status in the USA via obtaining a green card, a process that took several years, and my friend could seek alternative employment, she remained committed to this American family. No matter what other job opportunities came her way, she refused; she had to fulfill her promise to her employer and to the children. That was what loyalty meant to many people coming from the Caribbean, to work for Americans.

My friend and I shared many different stories about her babysitting experiences. I was invited several times over the years to her employer's home, to spend weekends or attend some celebration. My son, Miguel, and the two boys, Jeffrey and Danny became friends. I braided Erica's long, blonde hair, accompanied my friend to her swimming events, dropped her off at play dates, took her to Montgomery Mall, teased her about boys and every so often shared some of the same experiences my girlfriend lived. I witnessed how her employer depended on, trusted and needed her. Felicia devoted her life for more than fourteen years to her employers; they got the best of her. This was not a one way street. My friend was well paid, got bonuses, expensive gifts, and a self-contained room to which she retired each night.

Felicia started college at Howard University, since she wanted to leave her babysitting job with an education and be prepared to compete in the job market. Before graduating from college, even when she had not yet received approval for her resident papers, she still persisted at school, eventually completing her Bachelor's in Business. She made me proud of her, acknowledging the sacrifices she made in the USA, being a positive part of the cultural exchange.

My eighteen-year-old son is currently attending college in the City of Oneonta, about five hours away from New York City and his family. While he is now involved in an extended family and community of his own at Oneonta; the process of assimilation is still difficult. He has visited Trinidad and Tobago only once since his coming here eighteen years ago. All our relatives live in Trinidad; they have no intention of coming to the USA, except to visit. In many ways my son has missed out on the tradition of being Trinidadian. The little he knows is what we have passed on to him. In a recent conversation with him about his unfamiliarity with our local culture in Trinidad and Tobago, my son told me he didn't feel a sense of belonging to his homeland the way we do. He said he was glad to meet his family and extended families, but his life was in America.

His words sent a sharp arrow towards my heart; my son was now in a position to understand many things about life, and the choices his family made for him. From kindergarten through high school he gained a full Catholic education. He was now able to choose for himself. He shared with me his dreams about being a musician, finishing college, and going on to higher education. He told me he was thankful for the way his father and I raised him, and he appreciated the sacrifices we made in bringing him to a foreign land. But in making those sacrifices, we also paid the price of losing him to America. I was proud of my son, and the things we freely shared; all the things we are able to talk honestly about.

As I look forward to the day when our son becomes an American citizen, and gaze back to our first coming here, I feel a deep sense of pride and satisfaction. We have lived a good life, and while we have not accumulated wealth or achieved any form of societal status, we have done the best we could in raising a good and respectable son. His father has remained faithful to his education and upbringing, while I have been on my own trail pursuing dreams, my most profound joy has been watching him grow, encouraging, and holding his dreams up towards the sun.

The cloudless sky was darkening. There has been no promise of sunshine. This seems to be reflected on many sullen faces I walked past on 42nd Street. I got into the office at about 8:45 a.m. A few will be late; the rain being their excuse. For a moment I sat with the lights turned off. I relaxed. The telephone rang. I got up; turned on the light switch, "…may I help you?" A woman has just lost her passport, and wants to know what to do. I was not in the mood to talk, not quite awake. I asked her to please hold the line, and pushed the hold button. I closed my eyes, slowly rubbing my temples. Seconds passed. I opened my eyes again, picked up the receiver, and returned to the caller. I told her what she needed to know. I was not very patient with her line of questions. She got what she needed. I hung up. The morning rattled hard in my head. Folks began to come in "Good morning, how are you?" says one voice, then another, "Hi Sue, Good morning!" My day steadily crept forward.

Nearly two decades later since coming to the USA, separated by about two thousand, two hundred and three miles from my family, their dreams, and the day-to-day events of their lives, I seem to walk alone. Each day I travel. One, among thousands. In noisy train stations during rush hour whenever I stare into dull, empty eyes and lonely faces, I see my grandmother, just turned ninety-two, dressed nicely, red lips, rocking on her special chair, in the same gallery where warm sunlight catches bits of her frail face, and humming birds dance over wired fences, still singing, "How Great Thou Art".

At her age, my grandmother has grown too feeble to sing her favourite songs; her days are usually spent indoors lying upon her bed. In recent months she has fallen one too many times. She can no longer attend mass, and so three ladies trained in the Sacrament of the Holy Eucharist visit our home every Sunday morning to pray with her, and give her the Sacrament of Holy Communion. Three of my grandmother's sisters have passed away, the eldest, Tanti Ding Ding, Tanti Popo, and the last, Tanti June. My grandmother has only one sibling still alive, her older brother Uncle Harry who will turn ninety-five this year in October. In 2007 when I visited with my family, I was present when my grandmother's youngest sister, Tanti June passed away; she was eight-seven. I am thankful to have grown up with my family, who has taught me many things about living. My grandmother now eats like a baby, sometimes she says she has no appetite, and is unable to swallow anything. I am saddened by this image of my grandmother.

Recently, when I visited my grandmother I tweezed her stray grays, trimmed her hair before plaiting it in one tiny braid. She is as delicate as the kiskadees I see each morning. They sing at our back door. I feed them papaya and scraps of food. Sometimes they fly into the kitchen and land upon the table to greet me. Together, my grandmother and I shared cake and ice cream. Before dessert, I brought her lunch and prayed with her. Whenever I hugged her, I felt protruding ribs and fragile limbs. Waiting for death, yet hanging on to life, and being fearful about what comes after death cannot be an easy or simple transition. We don't talk enough about it. We are programmed to forget that eventually just as we have a chance at birth we might all have a chance at old age. Growing into older years of life, year after year deepens my responsibility to life and all the experiences I have been lucky to participate in.

I think of how lucky I am today to have the chance to experience American culture. Here, I see women as old and delicate as my grandmother boarding buses, trains, and shopping alone, carrying heavy bags, being pushed and shoved around. The other day it was reported on the news, a young man robbed and savagely beat two elderly women my grandmother's age. I become saddened by such occurrences. I think of how blessed my grandmother and I have been – that we both have been shaped and sheltered under the wide wings of four extraordinary men. Wings that were, at the same time, solid and soft. I think of how rare these qualities are, and how unique my circumstances were.

Memories of my life in Petit Valley rush past impolite stares, hard bounces and harsh gestures of the daily commute in New York City. They filter in and out my mind like hurried passengers beside me on a fast-moving train. They bounce, hit and nudge my senses. It is from here that I feel my Uncle Daniel's sturdy shoulders cradling me under our guava tree. Travelling home to Staten Island, on the ferryboat, in May, when cool air still makes the hairs on my skin rise, and a glint of the evening's sun softly flickers in the distance, I see images of a little girl, today, a woman – a small seed with strong roots planted years ago. With lovely branches spreading out far. Scattering blossoms. Reaching up.

A woman narrator who turns her small world upside down, is the kind of woman I'd like to be. She is made up of broken dreams and heartbreaks. She doesn't say much, but is filled with words. She dreams up life as if the world was made up of only women, women who are awake, alive and vibrant. She conjures magic in the circle of her hands. She owns nothing and wants to be owned by no one. She belongs to herself. She dances with the wild. She speaks her own language; she lives as if there were no tomorrows, and she cries. Her soft echoes vibrate throughout the universe; her tears wipe our pain free. She embraces our brokenness – our emptiness. She holds us strong inside her breasts. She is both man and woman. Her vision has no limit.

She understands the price for her freedom has been paid. She answers to the call of ancestors. She is rock and water. She is not afraid of imperfections; imperfections are man-made. Her flow is her own. Knowing is quite often secret, revelations, a choice. She talks, but also listens. Inspiration does not come from a single person, but from engagement with life. She is infectious. She is more than her lips, thighs, more than her breasts – what is unseen, untouchable, she is. She is more than her lovely face, her name. Om. Woman is simply a word to her; a word without meaning, for meaning has been tampered with.

A woman narrator who turns her small world upside down stands alone; she is comfortable in her skin, and believes in her purpose. She is unsure of outcome, but enthralled with possibility. A woman narrator who turns her small world upside down believes in everything. She lives in, and by silence. Silence obstructs. Silence builds. Silence controls. Silence takes away. Silence restores. She has learnt silence is often the better bet. A woman narrator who turns her small world upside down is necessary.

On a more recent visit to the islands of Trinidad and Tobago, and while visiting with my mother in Tobago, on one occasion, I had the chance of being the only person on the beach. This happened because it was a work day; early in the day, most people usually don't go to the beach during the week, except of course visitors. I was lucky. I started walking slowly along the beach feeling my feet sink into wet sand, watching my footprints disappear as waves caress the shoreline and splashed me until I was swept up in the moment.

On this particular day, while walking along the beach, I collected tiny stones. So I started collecting small stones every time waves crashed upon the shore and shifted sand beneath my feet. The stones were small and came in so many different shapes and sizes, each one telling a different story about its journey. The moment I gathered them inside the palm of my hand, and noticed the awesome variety, a wave quite unexpectedly lashed them out to sea. Off my feet, I stumbled to the ground only to realise it was my life – fragments of my life, I had been collecting just like tiny stones – bad experiences and moments of inbalance that were washed out to sea... People coming in and out of our lives; some die; friends betray; many good things also happen to us creating new balance. Then I started collecting more stones once again; they were new and beautiful. I understood many circumstances of my life – from a little girl into a woman – always beginning again.

The stones represented all the fragments of my life that came together, although over the years things shifted and life changed. These were valuable pieces of ever-changing memories, and while watching waves lap hard towards the shore, catapulting me, I knew as a writer the sand will always be shifting under my feet. On another occasion, my mother joined me on one of our walks together along the same deserted beach. That day she picked up a stone and handed it to me; it was the shape of a perfect heart, washed ashore. I was convinced each tiny stone was a necessary find, fragments of my life coming together to form the journey of my heart.